SPARKS
OF LIGHT

SPARKS OF LIGHT

Counseling in the Hasidic Tradition

Zalman M. Schachter
and
Edward Hoffman

SHAMBHALA

BOULDER & LONDON 1983

SHAMBHALA PUBLICATIONS, INC.
Horticultural Hall
300 Massachusetts Avenue
Boston, Massachusetts 02115
www.shambhala.com

Printed in the United States of America

Distributed in the United States by Random House, Inc.,
and in Canada by Random House of Canada Ltd

LIBRARY OF CONGRESS CATALOGING-IN-PUBLICATION DATA

Schachter-Shalomi, Zalman, 1924–
    Sparks of light.
    Bibliography: p.
    Includes index.
    ISBN 0-87773-240-X (pbk.)
    ISBN 0-394-72188-8 (Random House: pbk.)
    ISBN 1-57062-695-2 (pbk.)
    1. Hasidism—History.   2. Pastoral counseling (Judaism)—History.
    I. Hoffman, Edward.   II. Title.
BM198.S29   1983   83-42804
296.8'33
BVG 01

For Jonathan Gamliel and Alisa Joy

CONTENTS

SPARKS
OF LIGHT

PREFACE

IN RECENT YEARS, there has been a tremendous revival of interest in Hasidism. More works on this fascinating Jewish tradition are now being published in English than ever before. The range of these books has varied tremendously; many have recounted classic Hasidic stories and legends. Other writers have sought to describe something of the unique Hasidic way of life as it was initially practiced in Eastern Europe in the eighteenth and early nineteenth centuries.

Some of these narratives have noted the existence of the *yehidut*, or sacred encounter between hasid and rebbe, to solve the hasid's inner problems. However, no previous accounts of Hasidism have really examined in detail this intriguing relationship—especially its psychological implications. This fact is ironic, for Jews in that period lived harsh and oppressive lives; the *yehidut* was aimed not only at uplifting the individual spiritually, but emotionally and physically as well. It served a vital function in the Hasidic community. For to meet the needs of his hasidim, the rebbe often used techniques that were certainly psychotherapeutic by present-day standards. He was a counselor in the fullest sense of the term.

Moreover, with the shift in emphasis today from simply removing pathological symptoms to enhancing our total well-being, the model of rebbe and hasid is even more germane to us. It is clear that their mutual involvement expressed an

1

holistic perspective often lacking in mainstream, secular methods of understanding and treating inner disharmony.

Our objective in this book, therefore, is to shed light on this provocative dimension of early Hasidism. We plan to look at the types of rebbes who existed, for each typically manifested his own, particular approach to our universe within. Yet, because we have no precedents for this sort of exploration—and no primary sources establishing a "typology" of rebbes as counselors—we have drawn a "composite" or gestalt picture. We believe that this gestalt will provide a more lucid and still faithful image of how the Hasidic founders served as life-advisors.

In preparation of this work, we have relied mainly on written resources from the early Hasidic tradition. Such documents have included original philosophical treatises, anthologies of public discourses, anecdotal reports, and letters. We have also incorporated tales that have come down to us through word-of-mouth. While we have met with contemporary rebbes who actively make use of counseling, we have not emphasized their activities in the scope of this book.

To those with previous acquaintance with Hasidic literature, it will be evident that we have used language and modes of thought not always borne of the literature itself. We have done this to make more accessible Hasidic writings that would have otherwise proven quite opaque. In keeping with the aim of our work, our orientation to the material has encompassed two key avenues: first, we have sought to convey the rebbe's position as counselor—as seen from *within the Hasidic milieu.* Second, we have maintained a present-day focus to dramatize the relevance of Hasidic thought to the quest for wholeness and meaning in our lives.

To accomplish both of these goals, we have incorporated many Hasidic stories focusing on life situations. Such tales are very close to the heart of Hasidism and retain much of their original intensity. In translating these, we have tried to be as faithful as possible to the primary sources. And, as is true for the world's other great spiritual teachings, the Hasidic stories must be understood on many levels at the same time.

We feel personally well suited to this challenging task. Zalman M. Schachter was ordained as a Lubavitch-trained rabbi and for thirty-five years has brought the Hasidic way to men and women in the United States and abroad. He is currently professor of religion in mysticism and the psychology of religion at Temple University; he is cordially called the *zeyde* ("granddad") of the Jewish catalogue—*havurah* ("friendship") movement. He also heads the B'nai Or Religious Fellowship in Philadelphia. Edward Hoffman attended Orthodox *yeshiva* (Hebrew day school) as a child and received his doctorate in psychology from the University of Michigan. From his vantage point as a practicing clinical psychologist, he has in workshops around the country and in books such as *The Way of Splendor* demonstrated the exciting psychological insights found within the Jewish mystical tradition.

We hasten to stress that the Hasidic vision of our inner makeup far exceeds the boundaries encompassed by the space of this one book. We have endeavored to highlight the special, therapeutic aspects of early Hasidism; certainly, though, the source material can be richly mined for other purposes. And, while we believe that the Hasidic founders have a great deal to offer both helping professionals and interested audiences today, we have in no way intended to reduce this spiritual system to a modern, secular one.

If we have been able to spark the reader's own *yehidut* encounter with the rebbe within, our hopes will have been fulfilled.

est and encouragement, firmness and empathy, have kept the project from disintegrating. I am grateful also to Miss Mary-Lynn Paterson, my manuscript typist and editorial assistant, whose combined patience and insistance have led to many changes which have made the work more coherent. Finally, I owe a vote of thanks to my patient and long-suffering family.

Friday, February 11th—Yud Shvat 5727
Yahrzeit of my late Master
Rabbi Joseph Isaac Schneersohn z"l of Lubavitch

Eve of the Sabbath:
And the Lord goes before them,
A cloud by day to lead the Way,
A light beam by night to enlighten them.
So that day or night, they might go forward.
(Exodus 13:21)
Zalman M. Schachter

In their unflagging encouragement throughout the progress of this writing, I wish to offer thanks to my parents, brother, and especially to my wife Laurel. Gertrude Brainin and Dorothy Smith were also a constant source of support. Dr. Gerald Epstein and Aaron Hostyk provided me with many hours of stimulating conversation related to the topics discussed here. For their editorial enthusiasm, I would like to extend my gratitude also to Samuel Bercholz and Larry Mermelstein.
Edward Hoffman

INTRODUCTION

OUT OF THE GREAT SHADOWS surrounding East European Jewry in the eighteenth century, the Hasidic movement suddenly arose and burst into splendor. Beginning with the inner fervor of one man, later known as the Baal Shem Tov ("Master of the Good Name"), Hasidism spread like a fire of holy sparks across the *shtetl* landscape. Extolling the virtues of simplicity and joy, the Baal Shem Tov and his adherents eventually succeeded in winning over fully half of the Jews in Eastern Europe. Though this exuberant, experiential branch of Judaism seemed to wither with the rise of the Industrial Age, today there is an unprecedented resurgence of interest in early Hasidism.

For many Jews in those difficult times, life was harsh and oppressive. Economically and politically, they endured a bleak existence. They were also physically defenseless, dependent for sheer survival on the fickle whims of the feudal aristocracy. The Christian serfs themselves were treated little better than slaves; they were easily whipped into a frenzy of hatred against the Jews. Indeed, in the mid-seventeenth century, over half a million Jews perished in raids led by the Cossack chieftan Bogdan Chmielnitzki. Soon afterward, Sabbatai Zevi's disastrous messianic movement brought untold thousands of Jewish believers to utter ruin and despair.

Prior to the advent of Hasidism, too, the age-old religion lay non*kohen*—served as both legislator and advisor. Generally, these twin functions were tightly intertwined. The Laws were usually first issued to the Jewish people as simply good advice; only later, when sanctions were felt needed to motivate the unwilling, such guidelines were codified into Law. In fact, the very word Torah points to the task of "casting," that is, directing.

Still later in Jewish history, the spiritual master was more than merely the teacher of the Law; he was often regarded as a superhuman mediator. From the time of the prophet Elijah, an unbroken chain of precursors to the Hasidic rebbe appeared to the Jew in need—who "implored mercy and he was healed." The person who studied the Torah for its own sake was considered worthy of the gifts of the spirit; of such a sage it was said, "one can benefit from his counsel and be healed by him." This role made the Torah scholar into a holy guide, for "the secrets of the Torah are made known to him." Simultaneously, in his daily conduct, he was an accessible model to all.

In the Middle Ages, the great *zaddik* or righteous leader often functioned on two related levels at the same time. For instance, Rabbi Judah the Pious of Ratisbon was both an exemplar to large numbers of simple Jews and also a master of esoteric lore, a revealer of sacred mysteries. The charismatic sage, more so than the Talmudic scholar, acted as a popular counselor; reports of the sage's marvels brought him many followers.

In virtually all periods of Jewish counseling, the personal maturity of the postulant was reflected in the type of questions he posed. Each person was thus guided in a different manner. And, this tradition of advice-giving was nearly always an oral one. Whether a person sought formal instruction in the secret operations of the cosmos, or experiential, meditative techniques, there were few written works available. The postulant had to learn such supernal matters *B'yahid*, by being alone with a spiritual master. Perhaps that is why this special encounter between hasid and rebbe was called the *yehidut*.

Throughout history, Jewish mystics have taught that the

Biblical tale of Abraham's descent into Egypt must be interpreted on more symbolic levels as well as the literal one. In every generation, we are told, men and women must embark on their own journey for ultimate freedom from the "Egypt" within. Today, certainly no less than in previous eras, we are confronted with the reality of our darker impulses and the promise of awakening our more exalted potentials. The Hasidic tradition offers us a clear and welcoming path to reach the Holy Land.

CHAPTER ONE

THE HASIDIC WORLD

Man's main task in this world is to transform darkness into light. He must therefore raise up these Sparks, elevating them higher and higher until they return to their Root and Source.

—Rabbi Levi Yitzchok of Berdichov

In working with people to bring them to themselves, one must work at great depth, a depth scarcely imaginable.

—Rabbi Nachman of Bratslav

WHILE EARLY HASIDISM FLOWERED into something magnificently unique within Judaism, the Hasidic founders hardly existed in an historical vacuum. In responding to a way of life that had become tired and resigned, they brought a new vitality and exuberance whose energy we are still experiencing today. Like other great spiritual systems of the world, Hasidism manifested a wisdom transcendent of time and space;

13

the provocative ideas of its seminal leaders seem no less at home in our all-night cities than in the quiet countryside of Eastern Europe.

Certainly, men and women today still urgently seek the inner wholeness the Hasidic sages promised their contemporaries; our day-to-day problems about marriage, family, and livelihood are ultimately not much different from those brought to the rebbes for solution. Then, as now, people worried over their health and finances. Yet, it would be a mistake for us to lose sight of the particular historical and cultural forces that stimulated the rise of this charismatic Jewish movement. Indeed, our familiarity with *shtetl* conditions—even in general— will greatly enhance our understanding of the counseling methods which the rebbes developed. For this reason, we will briefly highlight the antecedents and origins of classic Hasidism.

VILLAGE LIFE

After the Chmielnitzkian massacres in 1648 and the disastrous messianic movement led by Sabbatai Zevi several years later, East European Jewry felt demoralized and hopeless. Many Jews were overwhelmed by a sense of isolation in an utterly hostile Gentile world. Evil seemed to be the reigning principle of the universe; the psychic atmosphere appeared thick with demonic invaders.

Nevertheless, life had to go on. In reconstructing their broken communities, Jews were obliged to settle in villages owned by the feudal aristocracy. For well into modern times, the surrounding local peasants were treated little better than slaves; periodically, the gentry encouraged them to vent their murderous frustration on their non-Christian bretheren. While Jews possessed a few privileges, these were all too soon revoked for failure to pay the rent on schedule. In fact, many Hasidic tales hinged on the problem a Jew faced in satisfying the landlord on time—and the ominous consequences that loomed for nonpayment.

With both political and spiritual salvation removed to the messianic future, East European Jewry found few outlets for their creative, inner strivings. To the intellectual elite, there was one key resource: study and debate over the Talmud. Such activity provided a reassuring purpose and structure to daily existence. In highly cerebral, refined *pilpul* discussions about exact Talmudic dicta and interpretations, scholars derived great comfort and meaning. They also enjoyed status for their mental abilities and a corresponding sense of self-worth. Furthermore, it should be recognized, for gifted Jews of the time—completely barred from attending the European universities—Talmudic study was virtually the only recourse for an inquisitive mind.

Unfortunately, the uneducated Jewish masses were unable to participate in this sort of conceptual luxury. Only a handful in each town could afford the necessary year of scholastic diligence for Talmudic mastery; the rest were all too aware of their intellectual shortcomings and their own unmet yearnings for accomplishment. It is not hard to imagine the generations of brilliant thinkers who died unfulfilled in this oppressive environment; we can only guess at their untold numbers.

Moreover, without access to the rarefied realm of Talmudic discourse, the vast majority of Jews were effectively without decision-making power in either religious or secular matters. The tight, hierarchial structure of the *shtetl* or village accorded the average person little authority to make moral judgments or to express new ideas; most had to accede almost wholly to their better educated neighbors and learn to suppress their thoughts and impulses. Such folk often became rigid and obsessive-compulsive personalities; they moved through their days with constant bitterness and frustration.

Yet, not surprisingly, some Jews were unable to keep bottled within such intense feelings. In the chronic dissociation

be bought." The popular *shtetl* saying was, "He is a good one; he takes." When the Czarist regimes began to conscript Jews into the Imperial Army—to serve as ill-equipped footsoldiers without hope of promotion through the ranks—the weak Jewish allegiance to the government became even weaker. During periods of manpower shortages, Czarist soldiers would literally abduct children from their parents to swell the military forces. Those who were fortunate enough to have survived a war often returned to their *shtetls* maimed and incapacitated for life.

THE RISE OF HASIDISM

Against this rather bleak social landscape, the Jewish people were thus ceaselessly confronted with their humiliating poverty and their exile from the Holy Land. The Diaspora had gone on for century after unrelieved century; something would soon have to change, for life was becoming unbearable for the East European Jewish masses. Slowly at first, then with greater stridency, the *shtetls* began to manifest a growing restlessness and crisis outlook.

Some dedicated rabbis, seized with the memory of Chmielnitzki's massacres of their pious ancestors, took to roaming the countryside. Abandoning their scant security, they traveled incognito to better carry out their mission—urging their fellow Jews not to lose hope, but to faithfully observe their God-given Law. Others journeyed as itinerant preachers throughout the *shtetls*; preying on fear, they warned more darkly of further nightmares of destruction unless the Chosen People repented of their evil deeds. Still others, Israel ben Eliezer (later known as the Baal Shem Tov or "Master of the Good Name") among them, searched for a new way to ignite the fervor of the Jewish people once again.

Little is known historically about this man, though legends
arose about him even before his death. Born around the year
1698 in the small village of Okup, near the Carpathian
mountains, he came from a family distinguished by neither
social status nor education. Israel's parents died while he was
still young, and apparently someone in the community took
him in and gave him a home. For several years, he served as a
teacher's aide and transported the children to and from the
synagogue school. Seeming physically coarse and uneducated,
Israel initially so disgusted his brother-in-law, a prominent
rabbi, that he urged his sister to divorce him. However, she
refused to do so, and the couple relocated to a remote village
in the Carpathian mountains. There, they eked out a bare
living close to nature. After some time, they achieved a reconciliation with the family and ran an inn in the town of
Medzyboz.

During this period, Israel ben Eliezer gradually became
known as a healer and a "miracle-worker." According to legend,
at the age of thirty-six, about the year 1734, he first revealed
his spiritual mastery to the world. We are told that he was a
Kabbalist par excellence and transmitted his provocative knowledge of the universe through tales and parables. His brother-
in-law allegedly became his first close supporter and served
as an important link between the Jewish religious establishment and the burgeoning mass movement that Israel had
begun to spark.

Traveling from village to village, he conducted healings,
laying-of-hands, and offered informal talks on humanity's true
relation to the transcendent. Articulating sophisticated mystical notions in the form of appealing folk stories, he presented
an optimistic, joyful view of human existence. Like some of
the great Kabbalists before him, he wrote no books; what we
know of his unique teachings has come down to us as parables
recorded by his disciples.

Each of us, the Baal Shem Tov ("Besht" in abbreviation)
emphasized, is capable of reaching the highest states of spiritual enlightenment; the gates of heaven lie open all around
us. Declaring that Talmudic study was only one path among

many to the divine, he insisted, "No two persons have the same abilities. Each man should work in the service of God according to his own talents. If one man tries to imitate another, he merely loses his opportunity to do good through his own merit." And, he stressed, the surest path to loftier awareness is through physical liveliness and inner devotion; sadness and self-pity distance us from the Holy Source.

Though the Besht's message of hope spread rapidly among the uneducated Jewish populace, he also attracted some of the finest scholars of the day. They were impressed with his charismatic mastery of mystical lore and his radiant personality. Legend has it that his intimacy with the esoteric tradition of Judaism was unequalled, due to his being taught by the teacher of Prophet Elijah, Ahiah the Shilonite. On many occasions, we are told, he exhibited paranormal powers such as clairvoyance, telepathy, and precognition. Several years before his death in 1760, he carefully selected and trained disciples who would succeed him in promulgating his teachings.

Within fifty years of the Baal Shem Tov's passing, the Hasidic ("Pious" in Hebrew) movement spread with such incredible rapidity that it won over half the Jewish populations of Russia and Poland, the great centers of Jewish life in the eighteenth and nineteenth centuries. The Besht's emphasis on bodily vigor and emotional spontaneity came like a sudden lifting of chains to the oppressed; Hasidism exerted a tremendous force of renewal among many Jews. In its first half-century of growth, Hasidism generated its greatest creative splendor and produced a veritable galaxy of brilliant thinkers. Major leaders such as Rabbi Dov Baer of Mezritch (1710–1772), Rabbi Schneur Zalman of Liady (1745–1812), and Rabbi Nachman of Bratslav (1772–1810), each attracted particular followings of admirers and disciples.

Of course, not all Jews were drawn to the Hasidic way of life. Some were quite displeased with the rejection of the Talmud as the sole avenue to inner exaltation. Especially in the region of Lithuania, the rationalist stronghold, opposition to Hasidism was strong and bitter. Led by such Talmudic giants as Elijah Gaon ("Great Scholar") of Vilna, such persons—called *Mitnaggedim* ("Opponents") by the hasidim—condemned the message of the Besht as heretical. The *Mitnaggedim* publicly burned Hasidic writings, forbade pious Jews to marry hasidim, and excommunicated Hasidic authorities. They even denounced rebbes like Schneur Zalman of Liady to the Czarist police and accused them of plotting to overthrow the government. But the sweeping movement could not be stopped.

Eventually, the hasidim and their erstwhile enemies reluctantly joined hands against a new and common foe, the secularist Jews who sought to convert outright to Christianity or to systematically "modernize" Judaism to fit the times. By the early decades of the nineteenth century, Hasidism had clearly won its place as a legitimate expression of the Jewish spirit. Yet, to gain such acceptance from the Talmudic-dominated establishment, Hasidism paid a price: namely, the suppression of its wilder and more exuberant outpourings of emotion. Perhaps inevitably, too, the fervor of the original movement dissipated as the Baal Shem Tov and his personal disciples passed from living memory into the distant realm of myth.

Early Hasidic practices that had once been spontaneous and existential thus became institutionalized; other aspects, such as the Besht's meditative techniques, were quietly dropped. Following the bloodlines of some of the initial leaders, Hasidic "dynasties" arose in Eastern Europe. More than a few rebbes acquired regal-like trappings, courtly entourages, and removed themselves like kings from their people. For these reasons, our focus in the sections to follow will be on the heyday of Hasidism, when its vigor and power were greatest.

RITES OF PASSAGE

Central to the lifestyle of early Hasidism was the notion of relationship. Each person who joined a Hasidic community entered a realm of involvement and reciprocity—to God and to humanity, to animate and even inanimate forms. For the Hasidic founders taught that every aspect of the universe— from the tiniest grains of sand to the most distant stars— contains holy sparks yearning to reunite with their original Source. In each act and thought, the hasid strove to liberate such fallen sparks back to the divine splendor; this was the special mission of every individual on earth, the Besht declared.

To accomplish this challenging and awesome task, the Hasidic sages preached, Jews indeed needed to observe the sacred Law. But, the Baal Shem Tov stressed, our outlook should be one of joy and excitement, not morose restraint. Furthermore, he emphasized, each stage of human life brings with it unique opportunities for spiritual advancement; within our mutual involvements with family and community, we can best find the path to the transcendent.

Thus, committed hasidim were expected to pass through a series of uniform rites of passage in their journey through this existence, on to the next. While the various Hasidic groups differed in their particular approach to some of these rites, in nearly all instances they elevated the rebbe as their chief guide and advisor. Through both impromptu and carefully orchestrated *yehidut* (spiritual counseling) sessions with his followers, the rebbe helped them transform the mundane into the sacred. Later in this book, we will focus on the *yehidut* with considerable attention.

In the sections to follow, we will therefore highlight the key stages of the hasid's life. Alas, because the historical literature* has been written almost exclusively from the male perspective, we have little documentation available relating the woman's corresponding social development. Generally, though, her concerns centered on issues involving child-rearing, family dynamics, and maintaining a proper Jewish home. Like her masculine counterpart, she received aid on such problems through the *yehidut*.

It should also be noted that while the early Hasidic sages clearly formulated these specific rites of passage for all followers, they did not seek to stifle individuality. Rather, the Hasidic leaders believed that on the firm foundation of their practices each person enjoyed the greatest opportunity to express what was most unique and precious within. Without such a solid structure to everyday life, they preached, people easily become confused and chaotic; the closely delineated Hasidic way of life was seen to allow for true self-development. Thus, in the famous parable to elucidate this point, Rabbi Zussya once expounded that when, at death, he would be summoned to the Heavenly Court, he would not be asked, "Why were you not like Moses?" but more relevantly, "Why were you not like Zussya?"

Generally, a hasid's position on the Hasidic hierarchy was determined by his particular age group, for each was typically associated with a corresponding set of responsibilities. Therefore, as the individual moved from one life-stage to the next, he experienced a related shift in his concerns. Such transitions might well have proven disturbing and even traumatic for the hasid were it not for his recourse to the rebbe's private counsel in the *yehidut*.

---

*The *Havurah* and women's movements have recently made contributions to rites of passage for women. See the *Jewish Catalogues* for some of these.

The Bokher

The first stage of adult life was that of the *bokher* (*bahur* in Hebrew), or unmarried man. Usually, at this phase, the hasid was a full-time *yeshiva* student distinguishable by special grooming and garb. In some *yeshivot*, he was not permitted to smoke tobacco until the age of twenty nor show an interest in women unless he was seriously contemplating marriage. He was expected to visit the *mikveh* (ritual bath) regularly, certainly after a nocturnal emission.

Undoubtedly, the life of a *bokher* required strong self-discipline and commitment. To assist him in behaving as a proper hasid, both the rebbe and the *mashpiyah* (yeshiva teacher) provided constant guidance and counsel. Without their help, the *bokher* would have been lost. Usually, his chief concerns encompassed the realms of Torah study, prayer, and vocational choice. While the rebbe's task was to lead the young man through these formative years—such as through special counseling—the day-to-day details of his supervision were entrusted to the *mashpiyah*.

During his *bokher* years, the young man had several occasions though to see the rebbe. First, he participated in a general *yehidut*, when he submitted his *kvittel* (note of petition), which constituted his official initiation as a committed Hasid. Even if the *bokher* had no specific questions or problems to discuss with his mentor, this *yehidut* was necessary. The rebbe himself raised issues about the young man's course of study, his general background, and his life's major events. He would offer the *bokher* concrete suggestions regarding those areas of his life that might require immediate resolution or strengthening of willpower.

If the young man came to this key *yehidut* with a specific dilemma, the rebbe would deal with it, though not always precisely how the *bokher* had anticipated. That is, the rebbe often viewed the manifest problem as merely symptomatic of some deeper, underlying conflict. At a later interview, the rebbe might counsel the *bokher* on "reparative work" for the misdeeds of his youth. Such offenses ordinarily included masturbation, violation of the dietary laws or Sabbath, and similar acts. Though the rebbe preferred to concentrate on spiritual matters, he was willing to discuss any of the *bokher*'s concerns.

The *bokher* had minimal social involvement with women until he was ready to seriously consider marriage. At that time, he typically would ask an older, married friend and his wife to introduce him to a suitable young woman. However, it should be stressed, the criterion for suitability was not that the *bokher* be delighted by her physical charms or her graces. Rather, the major issue was her willingness to join him in leading a Hasidic life, over which the rebbe would be the sole and final arbiter.

Once the *bokher* was introduced to the young woman, he did not dawdle, but was expected to reach a marital decision after three or four meetings. If he found her suitable as a bride, he might propose to her by saying, "Is it all right with you that we should ask the rebbe whether we ought to get married?" The rebbe was the supreme judge as to the appropriateness of the match; the *bokher* submitted without question to the rebbe's decision.

Legend has it that a father came to ask Rabbi Zvi Ziditchoiver regarding a match for his son. The sage at first covered his eyes, but very soon opened them and said to the father, "Right now, she is combing her hair and it is not fit for me to look at her. I will look at her later."

Having been primed with such tales celebrating the rebbe's clairvoyant powers, the *bokher* was certainly prepared to trust his spiritual mentor's judgment implicitly about the suitability of the proposed match. He knew that the rebbe saw his prospective bride not merely in her bodily allure, but also in her soul's inner radiance. After all, Jewish mysticism clearly endorsed the Talmudic dictum that forty days before each child is conceived, a proclamation in heaven is issued, decid-

ing who will be its future mate; the rebbe, it was said, had
special access to such celestial decrees.

Upon granting approval of the match, the rebbe then met
with the *bokher* to plan an auspicious wedding date. Studying
in conjunction with both his teacher and spiritual mentor,
the young man was now expected to understand the intricacies
of Jewish law regarding marriage—particularly its sexual
aspects. Both advisors typically stressed the difference in
outlook between man and woman, and the importance of
honest communication in all phases of marriage. On the eve
of the wedding, the rebbe often conducted a special counseling session with the *bokher*; together with offering his blessing,
the rebbe imparted specific advice about the intentions of the
act of lovemaking and clarified any nebulous features of the
teacher's discourses.

The wedding itself was preceded by a prenuptial *farbrengen*
(fellowship gathering) and together these events comprised
the rite of passage of the hasid from *bokher* to *yungerman*. At
the *farbrengen*, the young man and the group of peers with
whom he had been associated met with their teacher to discuss the meaning of the Jewish home and its opportunities for
holiness. The *mashpiyah* would also lecture on the mystical
notion of the "second descent of the soul" that a person
experiences in marriage. In addition, he would present traditional Jewish guidelines to adult sexuality and the significance of eroticism in the spiritual contract between husband
and wife.

The parents of the young couple typically arranged the
wedding itself, provided they were involved with the Hasidic
community. If this were not the case, the children were
guided by the instructions of the rebbe, for the wedding was
celebrated according to definite customs. The exuberant music was exclusively Hasidic; men and women rejoiced in
separate banquet halls and danced separately. All were encouraged to eat, drink, and dance with abandon, but an underlying seriousness lay behind such merrymaking.

The new groom would listen carefully as an older hasid
would ritually expound:

Why is it that we celebrate the mating of a male and a female? If that is such a great *simcha* (happiness), why don't we celebrate it when a cow is being taken to a bull? Obviously, we don't celebrate the animal part. But since the two souls, who have been united and were one before they descended to earth, have, after such a long time of separation, found each other again, this *simcha* . . . betokens and foreshadows the great *simcha* of the union between God and all of Israel, and the coming of the Messiah, which is likened to the consummation of the marriage.

For this reason, the young couple did not leave for a honeymoon immediately following the wedding; rather, for a week afterwards, they would celebrate the *sheva b'rakhot* ("seven nuptial blessings"), recited at the homes of their friends. Those who knew the bride and groom would feel a sense of joy about the union, but they also would convey their awareness of the sacredness of marriage—its duties and responsibilities—as well as its difficulties.

The Yungerman

With the start of his marriage, the former *bokher* now assumed a new and more prestigious position, that of the *yungerman*. In this capacity, he strengthened his relationship with the rebbe and gained increased status in the community. Typically, at this time, the *yungerman* turned to the rebbe for guidance concerning a vocational choice—unless the new husband was fortunate to have a wealthy father-in-law prepared to support him as a full-time scholar for the rest of his life, or for at least some years of financed study. In such instances, the wife ran all the business affairs while her husband perused the holy books.

Not surprisingly, the *yungerman* usually sought the rebbe's advice in matters relating to marriage, parenthood, and vocation. He might have felt guilty about expressing sexual desires for his wife, or experienced misgivings about his marital or vocational decision. Certainly, the *yungerman*'s newly acquired responsibilities as husband and breadwinner led to occasional longings for his earlier, more carefree *bokher* existence.

Perhaps the *yungerman*'s chief inner difficulty lay in balancing his familial and economic duties with those concerning prayer and religious obligations. No matter how committed to business activities, each Hasid was wholly obliged to devote at least an hour each day to absorb Hasidic teachings, besides his more general study of Judaism. He was also expected to pray in a *minyan* (quorum) three times per day; on Sabbath, the more contemplative services lasted most of the morning and some of the afternoon. At least once a month, the hasid considered it his duty to attend a *farbrengen* to rekindle the sparks of his inner fervor. Furthermore, he was expected to contribute with time and money to those enterprises that the rebbe endorsed.

As a result of such intense demands, the *yungerman* often experienced a very real conflict between his religious commitments and those to his family and vocation. This dilemma was an existential one in the path he had chosen and could not be evaded; in keeping with millenia of Jewish tradition, Hasidism firmly opposed the celibate way of life.

For the most part, the rebbe counseled the *yungerman* to place his religious obligations above those familial and vocational in nature; in our own vernacular, he had to learn to set priorities. However, in cases of serious disputes, the rebbe often sought ways to stabilize the *yungerman*'s conflicted family situation or insecure business, while at the same time enable him to fulfill his religious duties. For *shalom bayit*—peace in the household—was considered of immense importance.

The Ba'al Habayit

The next stage through which the hasid passed was that of the *ba'al habayit*, the householder. This transition from *yungerman* was not an abrupt change, but a gradual and subtle one. As such, it was not marked by any specific ceremony. After the *yungerman* had been married for several years and had achieved an obvious order in his familial and vocational affairs, he was regarded as a "householder."

The rebbe viewed such a man as a mature adult, very much involved in the day-to-day world. Perhaps, the hasid was financially secure or even wealthy; in any event, his participation in mundane matters necessitated certain counsels on the rebbe's part. For he had to remind the *ba'al habayit* as to his particular purpose on earth: the uplifting of the fallen sparks in his sphere of life.

Because of the householder's success in meeting the challenges of the material world, the rebbe depended on him for financial support and also for carrying out special and prestigious missions. The hasid's children were usually now able to care for themselves, and so, he had greater time to serve the rebbe in community affairs. Furthermore, the rebbe also advised the *ba'al habayit* not to reject as inherently sinful his vocational commitments—for such involvements were valued as offering unique opportunities for inner development and service. Reflecting his high status in the Hasidic community, the householder often led the congregation in Sabbath prayers.

The Elterer Hasid

When the Hasidic householder reached the stage of life when his children were financially ready to take his place, he was expected to spend the rest of his days as a renouncer of worldly obligations. He had passed from the *ba'al habayit* to the *elterer hasid* position.

In this capacity, the older hasid was often respected for his wisdom; he was almost likened to the rebbe himself. The younger members of his community revered him as a spiritual model and an esteemed advisor. Their popular saying was that, "Those who think they can be hasidim without having observed older hasidim are wrong."

Yet, the relationship between the elder and his more youthful counterparts was a reciprocal one, with mutual benefits. By engaging himself with the younger hasidim who emulated him, the elder gained inner fervor—for these "spiritually chosen" children were often more fulfilling to him than his own, biological children. Having discharged his familial and vocational obligations through a long and active life, he could at last become a true *yoshev ohel*, one who devotedly "sits in the tent of the Torah." In many instances, too, the elder hasid was knowledgeable in Kabbalistic practices and would pursue the dazzling insights of Jewish mysticism; to be able to concentrate fully on the divine mysteries was truly the fruition of all of the hasid's prior acts—and preparation for the World to Come.

While the elder hasid occasionally sought his mentor's counsel, the rebbe at times relaxed formalities when meeting with him. After all, the rebbe regarded the elder as one who had advanced to a high rung indeed on the Hasidic hierarchy. And, with few exceptions, the problems for which the elder requested guidance concerned his children and grandchildren, rather than his own, unresolved internal conflicts. Such difficulties had usually been settled many years before.

In short, the early Hasidic way of life required a lifetime of dedication; it was not one that could be easily assumed. The Hasidic founders viewed inner growth as akin to climbing an infinite ladder; through daily tasks and responsibilities, in a careful, patient manner, one eventually reached the heights. Therefore, they ritualized counsel—in the form of the *yehidut*—to help each person master these forementioned stages of earthly existence.

To summarize, the hasid as a *bokher* was supposed to learn how to order his life in accordance with his physical, mental, and spiritual endowments. He had to realistically assess his inherited talents and weaknesses, and he needed encouragement for this often difficult, painful task. Later, as a *yungerman*, the young man required the rebbe's aid in accepting the realities of marriage, family, and vocation. He depended on practical guidance to balance the exigencies of the material world with those of the transcendent. Still later, as a *ba'al habayit*, he had to be reminded neither to forget his higher purpose on earth nor to disparage his mundane involvements. Finally, as an elder hasid whose bodily strength was waning, he needed advice to use his last years wisely, preparing for his physical death, and making a smooth transition to the World to Come.

Thus, the rebbe's challenging mission was to appropriately steer the hasid through each of life's major straits of activity. While repeatedly indicating to his congregants that this universe is but a tiny glimmer of the divine splendor, the rebbe simultaneously stressed the importance of each human deed and thought. For as the *Zohar* had aptly stated, "The way to the undisclosed is through the disclosed."

THE IMMORTAL SOUL

It is crucial to realize that the Hasidic universe of discourse resembled an iceberg; the Besht and his disciples ceaselessly taught that the world perceived through human senses is only a small fraction of the true cosmos. In fact, the rebbe—later called "the geologist of the soul"—directed most of his work toward these hidden regions. For the early Hasid, the mere fact that such realms are beyond ordinary sensation did not at all render them nonexistent. While in our own era, mainstream medicine and therapy take place against a secular and materialist backdrop, in the Hasidic milieu a spiritual outlook predominated. In fact, the vital *yehidut* encounter would have been meaningless—except on the level of simple advice—if metaphysical concepts were not inextricably interwoven.

To adequately summarize the vast mystical cosmology of Hasidism would draw us far outside the scope of this book. For an introduction to this fascinating subject, we recommend our earlier works on the Kabbalah (*Fragments of a Future Scroll* and *The Way of Splendor*). However, because a short recapitulation may prove helpful, we will examine some of the key mystical concepts most relevant to Hasidic counseling.

In essence, the Baal Shem Tov and his adherents adopted classic Kabbalistic ideas and promulgated these in the form of appealing folk stories and legends. They taught that every human comprises several distinct but interrelated attributes: those pertaining to physiological instincts (*nefesh*), social functions (*ruah*), and spiritual capacities (*neshamah*). While everyone makes use of their lower impulses in day-to-day life, the sages explained, many people rarely utilize their higher, more exalted potentials. Yet, these exist within all men and women. As the *Zohar* stated, "These three grades (*nefesh, ruah,* and *neshamah*) are harmoniousy combined in those ... who have the good fortune to render service to their Maker." Some Hasidic thinkers taught that within the soul two yet loftier dimensions—named *hayah* and *yehidah*—also operate, but at levels far beyond those of the mundane world.

Many rebbes prescribed specific meditative techniques to awaken the intuitive, creative side of the mind; they also recommended dreams and chants as especially powerful tools to achieve higher consciousness. Thus, they urged their followers to examine their dreams carefully for inner messages. Rabbi Dov' Baer of Lubavitch, speaking of melody, observed, "Each soul can only ascend to the root of the Source whence she was hewn by means of song."

Above all, the Hasidic leaders stressed that every soul is linked to realms wholly transcendent of time and space. While the Besht and his disciples extolled the wonders of the cosmos and of nature, they insisted that this existence is ultimately but a dark, narrow passageway to hidden worlds of ineffable radiance. Each person on earth is here to accomplish certain definite goals, the Baal Shem Tov expounded; through involvements with family, friends, and others, one fulfills this purpose. And, when such goals are finally accomplished, it is time to move on—to greater challenges and opportunities, to ever-increasing closeness to God. As the Lubavitch founder poetically wrote, "Each spark descended into this world—indeed a profound descent and a state of true exile—to be clothed in a body and vital soul ... so as to join and unite them with the Light."

Thus, the Hasidic sages urged their followers not to fear bodily death, but to meet their impending physical end with full tranquility and lucidity. The hasidim regarded the act of dying as an event of transition—and of initiation—into the supernal realms. For this reason, they often compared the pangs of birth, the pangs of death, and the pangs of the waiting Messiah as akin to one another. Nevertheless, they taught, for those properly trained, dying is hardly more difficult than "removing a hair from the milk," or walking through one door into a larger chamber. The Hasidic masters emphasized that death's inner pangs arise from one's degree of attachment to the lures of the material world.

From its inception, therefore, Hasidism incorporated deathbed scenes as important illustrative lessons; frequently, such tales included specific melodies to learn. For example, we are told that on his deathbed the Besht encouraged his disciples to sing a special tune of his; he promised to return and pray with those who would chant it with complete absorption and devotion. As he lay dying, he calmly—in a step-by-step fashion—explained precisely how his soul was embarking toward loftier realms. Continuing to pray and teach, he finally closed his eyes and said, reciting the Psalm verse, "Do not bring me to the foot of pride."

In a related story, a pious hasid lay on the verge of death. As his friends assembled around him, he methodically instructed them how to sing a new melody he had composed; when they had learned it sufficiently to carry the tune among themselves, he leaned back and smiled, and died.

The Hasidic founders often discoursed on the quality of life necessary for a mystical, ecstatic death, which they compared to a "divine kiss." Some rebbes recommended definite meditations to attain this wondrous experience; they even conducted exercises in "simulated dying." Intriguingly, they regarded the third, final meal of the Sabbath as a microcosm of human mortality, for an additional, higher soul was said to come and then depart on each passing Sabbath. Thus, the rebbes presented during the sacred, dwindling Sabbath hours their talks and experiential techniques concerning death.

Rabbi Bunam of Pshiskha taught that those who prepared themselves for sleep as if they were about to die would find the final journey just as easy. He based his lesson on the Talmudic dictum that nightly sleep is a sixtieth of death. In one of the most beautiful of all Hasidic tales, Rabbi Bunam lay dying as his wife sat beside him and sobbed with grief. He thereupon turned to her and said, "Why do you weep? All my life has been given merely that I might learn how to die."

To reduce their dependency on the material world, the early hasidim employed rigorous methods of mental purification. For instance, we are informed that the renowned Rabbi Barukh of Medzyboz once deliberately shamed a man in public. A colleague who visited Rabbi Barukh took offense and said, "Is it not written that he who shames his fellow in public has forfeited his after-life?" Rabbi Barukh thereupon replied, "If this is what he needs to be helped, it is my duty to forego my reward in the World to Come for the sake of my hasid." In this case, the great sage had to transcend a normally gentle relationship with his disciple to protect his livelihood; both rebbe and hasid together therefore underwent a kind of liberating social "death."

JOURNEY THROUGH THE BEYOND

Hasidic masters delineated several orderly stages that characteristically follow the experience of dying. They saw no sharp breaks in continuity from this universe to those realms beyond space and time; only the limited human consciousness creates such false distinctions. As the *Zohar* clearly noted, "It is the path taken by man in this world that determines the path of the soul on her departure."

Hasidim believed that the earthly soul is summoned to appear before the Heavenly Tribunal and required to recount all of its deeds, words, and even thoughts from the course of its life; rebbes deemed this stage a prerequisite for the more exalted ones to follow. However, we are told, some souls are stricken with a sort of amnesia from the shock of death—due to their intense identification with the material world—and hence, cannot remember their identity when brought to the Heavenly Tribunal. To prevent this occurrence, some rebbes taught mnemonic devices designed to help their hasidim recall their Hebrew names at the crucial time.

Next, some souls must undergo a *hibut haqever* or "beating

of the grave." Most persons cannot imagine having an identity separate from their physical being. Such earthboundedness
must be let go before the soul can ascend to higher regions.
For some, the disintegration of their bodily form is emotionally painful; still, they must undergo this process until all
gross sensual identifications have been surrendered. Based on
this notion, the Hasidic founders stressed the significance of
self-discipline and self-control over one's instincts—so that
people can discover while still alive that they comprise another,
spiritual Self to the physiological one.

After the "beating of the grave," each soul must next be
cleansed of other physical vibrations. Since men and women
are usually driven by their urges and desires, by all the
syllables and sounds they have heard, these noises are said to
resound like clanging coins in a gourd within their innermost
being. Until such cacophony is stilled, they are unable to
absorb the vastly more subtle, divine harmonies in the higher
spheres. Thus, we are told, two angels at either end of the
universe toss and rattle the soul from one side of the cosmos
to the other—in a *kaf haqela* or "catapult"—until all the accumulated psychic dust has been filtered away. When this severe process is accomplished, the soul no longer need wander
from illusion to illusion, surrounded by the confusion (*tohu*)
of its own sensory images and desires. In one illustrative
Hasidic story, a *dybbuk* who had roamed for eons in this lonely
void cried out, "Would that I had already reached Gehenna."
For to attain Gehenna or Purgatory, the soul must first be
shaken of its earthly attachments.

The Baal Shem Tov and his disciples advised that people
can, in everyday life, experience the purifying state of *kaf
haqela* through deep meditation. They prescribed a variety of
sophisticated mental techniques, such as following thoughts
back to their point of origin in consciousness. In this manner,
persons could advance more easily in their journey to the
inner Source. Yet, the early hasidim recognized the inherent
difficulty in truly calming the mind. As the Besht himself
observed, "This is one's constant work in the world."

According to Hasidic tradition, no Jewish soul can remain

in Purgatory for more than twelve months; Abraham stands guard at its gates and frees those who have completed this period. Though the rebbes often described Gehenna with lurid physical details of searing fires and chilling ice, they indicated that this region is ultimately a spiritual condition. They taught that Gehenna exists simply to cleanse inner stains caused by sins that still cling to the soul after the "catapult" experience. Emphasizing that in this phase souls learn to relinquish their most tenacious earthly desires, they stressed that God had intended no form of revenge. Rather, this process was a purging that felt blissful afterwards.

Upon completing these prior stages of purification, each soul stands ready to enter into the various levels of *Gan Eden* ("The Garden of Eden") or Paradise. But the soul must first go through one more realm of preparation: immersion in the River of Light that flows out of the "pores" of the Heavenly Host as they sing praises to the Highest One. This immersion frees the soul from its last, remaining physical images—even those good in themselves—so that it can experience heaven as it really is.

In their sacred ablutions in the *mikveh* ("ritual bath"), the early hasidim practiced an earthly counterpart to this exalted state. They regarded the four walls of the *mikveh* as symbolic of the four letters of the mysterious Divine Name; by dipping four times into the *mikveh*, the hasid surrendered wholly to the supernal energies of the Divine Mother.

At last, we are told, the soul flies to its appropriate station in *Gan Eden*. There, it joins the company of other souls with whom it feels inwardly closest. Just as on earth, each soul gravitates towards its most comfortable level. The *Zohar* succinctly states, "For there are many abodes prepared by the Holy One, blessed be He, each one according to his grade. . . . As the works of the righteous differ in this world, so do their place and lights differ in the next world." Or, as the Maggid of Mezritch tersely explained, "Each man creates his own Paradise."

The higher the reaches of *Gan Eden*, the greater the unshielded, Infinite Splendor of God can be felt. In Paradise, each soul thus continues its upward climb of knowledge and devotion, but inexpressibly nearer to the divine brilliance and oneness of all. Typically, the Hasidic sages have refrained from attempting to describe this state of existence, for mere words obviously fail. But their central image is one of Light, an endless dazzling radiance that bathes the soul in unspeakable rapture and ecstasy. The *Zohar* tells us, "The primal point is the innermost light of a translucency, tenuity, and purity passing comprehension."

Eventually, the Besht and his adherents taught, the soul absorbs all it can in Paradise before it must return to this realm for another lifetime. Though many souls bitterly protest and cry out at the summons to be reborn, they are obligated to return to this vale of tears in order to complete their unfinished tasks. Misdeeds must be rectified; omitted acts must be carried out. No matter how lofty, every soul must reincarnate to make such corrections, to uplift all of its surrounding sparks of light. For all the countless worlds of creation are interrelated; the slightest happening in one realm ripples through all the others.

But, the Hasidic masters preached, men and women were not alone in their awesome mission to unify Creation. Their rebbe stood waiting to comfort them, to inspire wisdom, and to show them the paths back to the spheres of glory.

THE REBBE'S VOCATION

From the bird's-eye view we have presented of the early Hasidic milieu and outlook, it is clear enough why the *shtetl* folk sought the rebbe's counsel. Certainly, they venerated him as a superior being, the intermediary between the earth and the very heavens. Poor, uneducated, and beleaguered by a hostile Gentile world, many East European Jews not surprisingly turned to the figure of the rebbe to lead them through the travails of daily life. But what was the rebbe's motivation? If he had experienced true enlightenment, why would he bother with mundane concerns about marriage and family, health, or livelihood?

Within Hasidism, the great sages themselves dealt extensively with this key question. One explanation they offered was that prior to embarking on higher meditative quests, pious Jews had always felt obliged to enter into a convenant with God. That is, before experiencing the sealed mysteries of the transcendent, they would vow to carry their visions back to the realm of everyday existence—with all of its distresses—in order to uplift others. Thus, the Hasidic founders stressed that the rebbe was simply continuing the age-old Jewish practice of blending the ecstatic with the pragmatic to exalt the people.

Secondly, the Hasidic masters were strongly convinced that their followers needed flesh-and-blood models to emulate. Still tainted by the legacy of the false messiah Sabbatai Zevi, many ordinary Jews naively believed that the spiritual illumination was manifested only in hysterical-like symptoms, or worse, in emotional disorder. To such Jews, a person's visible loss of inner control was somehow a sign of his or her holiness. While the *dybbuk* represented the power of confusion and uncontrolled passion, the Jewish populace generally lacked contrasting examples of genuine, sacred spontaneity. By observing the rebbe's daily, seemingly trivial activities, each Jew could therefore learn what wholeness and purity were really like. In a famous illustrative parable, a hasid once declared that he had traveled to a distant rebbe not to simply watch him pray, "but to see how he ties his shoelaces."

In Hasidic teachings, the rebbe was also seen as a very real intercessor for the bulk of the Jewish people. Through his enlightened mental state and his secret Kabbalistic skills to reach the supernal regions, he was considered able to influence even the Almighty to alter celestial judgments. Indeed, the rebbe was above all committed to the "sanctification of His Name." No task which would bring about the greater glorification of the Deity was deemed too inconsequential to undertake.

Consequently, the rebbe would not hesitate to seek miracles if these would help increase human belief in divine guidance. While the rebbe would refuse to act merely for earthly motives, he would gladly accede for this loftier purpose. In one relevant anecdote, Rabbi Mendel of Rymanov was once approached by a Gentile woman who asked him to heal her ailing son. Rabbi Mendel replied, "Why do you visit me? Do you think that I am a wizard?" When the anxious mother protested that she had come to him because of his closeness to God, he agreed to pray for the child's life. In other words, all was done for the true "santification of His Name."

Finally, Hasidism taught that the rebbe often took on his role to make amends for his own past misdeeds in earlier lives. According to legend, the Baal Shem Tov himself had attained the highest levels of consciousness under the tutelage of the prophet Elijah. But because the Besht, in this previous lifetime, in humble self-effacement thought himself unworthy of sharing his knowledge with others, he had been required to return, "so that the world would be filled with his fragrance."

So, too, with any rebbe. In order to atone for sins commited in prior existence—perhaps selfishly hoarding his divine revelations—the rebbe was seen to have reincarnated in order to aid his followers in their search for wholeness. Therefore, the disciples of the Great Maggid of Mezritch declared that those among their colleagues who had *not* become rebbes were actually the most pious souls.

In the early Hasidic milieu, the rebbe saw his life-task as the raising up of the fallen sparks everywhere. Having experienced the spheres of transcendence, he knew the purpose of his present incarantion as well as his past endeavors. As a result, he was able to diagnose his followers' problems and counsel them according to their inner needs. In helping his hasidim, he ultimately helped himself. In serving the Holy One, he fulfilled his own destiny.

CHAPTER TWO

JEWS IN NEED

Once there were a father and son who had been separated for a very long time. Each one greatly yearns for the other. Eventually, the father decides to visit his son. At the same time, the son makes up his mind to visit his father. They begin traveling toward each other, and as they come closer, their yearning grows all the more.

They continue traveling toward each other until they are separated by just a few short miles. The father begins to feel such great longing for his son that he realizes that he will not be able to endure it for the last few miles. The son also realizes that he can no longer endure his emotions. If he continues for the last few miles, he will be so overcome by them that he will literally die. They both decide to cast aside their yearning and put it out of mind.

Just at that moment, a coach comes along and swiftly brings the son to his father. Imagine the tremendous joy that the driver brings both father and son. . . .

God has a great longing for the Zaddik, just as the Zaddik yearns to return and come close to God. . . . A Jew brings the Zaddik his livelihood, and therefore brings him close to God.

—Rabbi Nachman of Bratslav

IN MANY WAYS, the institution of Hasidic counseling reflected like a glittering crystal Jewish life in Eastern Europe two centuries ago. It was an age before science and specialization; among the impoverished *shtetl* folk, daily conditions were

41

harsh and oppressive. It would be no exaggeration to say that for many Jews the rebbe's advice made the difference between hope and despair, joy and unrelieved depression. A word of comfort or inspiration, a surprising gesture of kindness, a blessing followed by an uncanny coincidence—such acts all served to elevate the hasid to a new, more exalted state of mind.

Moreover, this intriguing relationship was in essence a holistic one. The rebbe characteristically strove to harmonize each person's life; as a catalyst for inner change, he sought to induce a healthy balance between the forces of the material and spiritual worlds. Every man or woman in search of wholeness within had to learn this challenging task in a manner personally appealing and meaningful. For this reason, the *yehidut* was no simple, uniform procedure; its content mirrored the specific qualities of each rebbe and supplicant.

Certainly, the kinds of problems for which *shtetl* Jews requested counsel encompassed a multitude of concerns. Childless couples desperately begged for the gift of life, or else, solace for their unhappy fate. Struggling businessmen, weary of the never-ending battle to support their families, welcomed practical advice on improving their lot. Those physically ill, not unexpectedly, wished for a speedy recovery to health; those stricken by loss of faith and self-defeat hoped for a path to appear once more.

Just as the people's needs were many, so too were there many types of Hasidic rebbes. Some became renowned for the power of their intellect to cut through the tangle of one's conflicted life. From the sheer clarity of their thought, they could swiftly penetrate to the heart of the hasid's conflict and render superb guidance. Other rebbes were famous for their gifts of spiritual discernment and their capacity to see one's innermost soul in all its naked splendor. Still others were revered as spiritual healers, singers and storytellers, and adroit arbitrators.

In the sections to follow, we will examine some of the typical problems for which Jews of the time sought the rebbe's counsel. We will also look at the varied roles of the rebbes in their day-to-day activities, raising the holy sparks of the cosmos. For as Rabbi Isaac Kalov aptly remarked, "When you find one who can take out your innards, wash them, and replace them—while you are still alive—you have found your rebbe."

MEETING THE PEOPLE'S WANTS

From Darkness to Light

Despite their keen awareness of the transcendent, the Hasidic founders acutely recognized the realities of daily life. Indeed, their central message of joy and inspiration was that seemingly ordinary affairs are ultimately linked to the highest reaches of God. An apparently trivial act carries with it untold influence, they taught; a single commonplace deed or word may exert incalculable effects upon the world. From this perspective, the rebbe endeavored to help his hasid not only with exalted matters, but with more mundane ones as well.

Yet, observing that earthly life is only a small part of the whole, the rebbe did not wish his hasid to deal only with worldly concerns. Through subtle and sometimes not-so-subtle remarks, the rebbe usually made it plain enough where his greatest interest lay. Thus, at times, the hasid attempted to mask his true problems—about his marriage or earning a living—and instead talk about pious or lofty topics. By playing up to his mentor's obvious expectations, the hasid often was unaware how he unconsciously camouflaged his difficulties. However, the skillful rebbe soon brought his hasid's "hidden agenda" directly to the fore.

Among the most critical of earthly problems for *shtetl* folk was that of child rearing. Beyond it being a matter of reli-

gious obligation for them, Jewish couples attached tremendous existential significance to producing children, especially
sons, who would recite the mourner's Kaddish after their
parents' demise. For many centuries, Jews had looked to
divine intervention for such blessing; as far back as Biblical
days, when Elisha had promised a son to the Shunemite
woman, the tradition of the holy man's blessing had been kept
alive. Consequently, *shtetl* folk eagerly sought the rebbe's power
in this sacred realm.

For many Jews in that period, the desire for male children
was supreme. When it happened that a rebbe reported that,
in order to beget, a parent might have to suffer physically or
actually die, hasidim readily agreed. Indeed, according to
legend, the Hussyattiner rebbe and the father of the Komarnoer
offered their lives in order to have children. Furthermore, the
continuity of Jewish family life depended on the presence of
surviving, adult children. "Barrenness" even constituted valid
grounds for divorce. Despite these facts, though, the rebbe
had to be convinced of the parents' higher motives—to better
serve God—before proceeding with a blessing. If they simply
desired the status of siring male offspring, he turned them
away.

Village inhabitants also came to the rebbe for his prowess
as a healer. They typically hoped that his blessing alone
would effect the cure, though they tended to feel more reas-
sured if he also provided a magical amulet or *s'gulah*. Following the seminal practices of the Besht, some Hasidic leaders
even prescribed herbal remedies to alleviate their followers'
distress. They also engaged in touch and laying-on-of-hands.
Those who were physically ill wanted the rebbe's spiritual
guidance, too, for they were faced with a dilemma: in Jewish
law, a sick person is free from obligation to observe *mitzvot*,
yet the purpose of life requires their fulfillment. Hasidim
believed that failure to carry out *mitzvot* necessitated penitence or even another earthly incarnation. Thus, the rebbe
was needed to personally clarify the extent of one's religious
obligations.

Interestingly, the rebbe would not always agree to heal. He

sometimes suggested that the hasid bear the burden of ill health—to gain greater redemption later on, or to strengthen weak inner faculties. For example, when the ailing Rabbi Dov Baer, the Maggid of Mezritch, visited the Baal Shem Tov, Rabbi Dov Baer's overt goal was to become physically well again. Yet, we are told, "If the Besht had wanted to [simply] cure him, he could have. Even the Maggid himself could have performed the cure, but there was reason for not doing so." In other words, hasidim viewed sickness as secondary to more important issues.

Just as the barren were likened to the dead, so too were the poor. Certainly, alleviating the poverty of *shtetl* Jews was well within the primary domain of the rebbe. Offering his blessing, counsel, and specific advice, he strove to aid the hasid who lacked sustenance. For to pay the rent and taxes on time was a continuous struggle for many people. When a Jew was thrown into prison for nonpayment of rent, the rebbe often became the key figure in securing the necessary ransom for the individual's release. On many occasions, the rebbe also would raise money for destitute families. According to legend, the Baal Shem Tov and others personally carried out menial tasks of labor—like woodcutting and fire kindling—for the poor and helpless.

Some rebbes, though, were well known for *not* wanting to help their hasidim escape the clutches of poverty; a few such leaders even prayed for their own children to remain forever penniless, so that they might be wholly dependent on God's benevolence for daily survival. However, this sort of attitude was not common. Most rebbes showed great concern for the material welfare of their struggling hasidim.

In all of these cases of need, whenever the rebbe appeared to be successful, his followers eagerly spread the news throughout the countryside. Such tales brought many supplicants, each searching for divine assistance with the hardships of his or her life. In fact, as the Hasidic movement grew, the wonder-working abilities of the *Zaddik* ("righteous one") became so magnified out of proportion that some rebbes explicitly warned against this trend as a sign of spiritual degeneration.

A hasid once told the Kotzker leader about another rebbe who was credited by rumor with the power to work miracles. "I would like to know," said the Kotzker, "if he is able to perform the miracle of making one a real hasid."

The Social Agenda

In instances of personal conflict, many people solicited the rebbe's counsel. Husbands and wives, parents and children, in-laws and business partners—all came to obtain an equitable settlement and a reconciliation. On occasion, though, hasidim frankly asked the rebbe to rule completely in their favor—and persuade their recalcitrant spouses, parents, or children, or business associates, to simply give in—without a mutually satisfying solution. Of course, the rebbe was much less likely to carry out such wishes. Gentiles too relied on the rebbe to settle disputes among themselves or resolve disagreements involving Jews. Some Gentiles also requested the rebbe's blessing and advice concerning their children, health, or livelihood.

The needs of the villagers were manifold. Merchants desiring a tip on buying or selling sometimes came to the rebbe; they aspired to receive some useful business advice, perhaps regarding relations with customers or suppliers. Partnerships were formed and dissolved at at the rebbe's court and legal matters adjudicated. On occasion, a rebbe would rule in a case and afterward assist the loser by giving or lending him the money to fulfill his obligation. Financial worries not only encompassed the realm of livelihood, they endangered even marital matches—such as when the bride's father became unable to pay for the wedding and remit the dowry. To whom else could one then turn but the rebbe?

Furthermore, such urgent problems as forced conversion to Christianity and the abduction of children by the local gentry and clergy brought hasidim to their rebbe. They hoped too

that his miraculous intervention might enable their youngsters to escape the draft into the Czarist Army, for even little
children were subject to Imperial decrees. *Shtetl* folk had also
to contend with Jewish informers to the government; such
spies could provoke nightmarish havoc to the community.
Thus, hasidim sought the rebbe's protection against such
informers.

Tragic cases of abandonment were also taken before the
rebbe. Forsaken wives pleaded for him to locate their absconded husbands, so that either a divorce or a reconciliation
could be achieved. Childless widows, bound by the levirate
law to marry their brothers-in-law, came for aid in finding
them. In situations where the brother-in-law had become legally incompetent, these widows solicited release through the
rebbe's paranormal intervention. And, just as the Biblical
Saul had visited the prophet Samuel for counsel about the
lost donkeys, so too did villagers seek the rebbe's divine wisdom to locate lost objects or missing people.

The Spiritual Realm

For Jews of Eastern Europe two centuries ago, the forces of
evil seemed everywhere. In the supernatural as well as the
natural world, therefore, the rebbe's support was enlisted.
Hasidim who experienced themselves as having been hexed
had to combat local witchcraft, which they at times associated with the Christian clergy; the rebbe's function was to
render such demonic threats impotent. He also conducted
exorcisms of incubi and succubi. In cases of possession, he
relied on his merit and Kabbalistic acumen to heal or drive
away the troubled *dybbuk*. *Shtetl* folk even sought the rebbe's
help to favorably influence the forces of weather, for more
benign seasons usually heralded improved economic conditions.

Yet, to the rebbe himself, spiritual counseling entailed far
more than simply offering protection against hostile elements

in the universe. The rebbe compassionately treated all the wants of his hasid. But as spiritual mentor, he most longed to guide the hasid's inner growth—to awaken ecstasies, to teach him the way of splendor. Fortunately, many hasidim desired precisely this knowledge. As willing participants in the Hasidic community, they wished to intensify their fervor and devotion. For such persons, all social and economic matters were secondary to the task of joyfully serving the Holy One.

As the Baal Shem Tov had expounded and demonstrated, a living master was needed for real, inner development. Books alone could not suffice. Hasidim knew that the holy commandments relating to the emotions—what the eleventh-century Spanish sage Bachya ibn Paquda had called "the duties of the heart"—had no Talmudic treatises that discussed these in detail. Thus, in the striking image of the Berdichover, the rebbe himself was to be the tractate of Divine Love and Awe.

The rebbe signified not only the manifest territory of the Torah; he also provided a map to its hidden, exotic regions. Many hasidim would listen for hours while their rebbe initiated them into the sacred mysteries of *Hasidut*, the innermost realm of the Torah. They yearned to hear the constantly issuing voice from Sinai. No one but the rebbe could awaken such acuities. However, despite the lofty matters—"the secrets of heaven and earth"—that the rebbe shared with his hasidim, his emphasis always centered on *avodah* and good deeds, and not on metaphysical indoctrination. As Rabbi Nachman of Bratslav explained, "The chief goal of understanding is to know God in our heart, not in our brain. The heart is conscious of fear and awe, and induces [one] to pure service."

Penitents seeking a prescription for atonement constituted a basic part of the rebbe's ministry. Rebbes often vied for the honor of the epitaph, "Many did he turn from sin." Whereas in the past, penitents had been treated to a standard set of guidelines in order to rectify their misdeeds, the Hasidic founders sought to treat the sinner and not his symptoms. Some rebbes were renowned as "specialists" in this capacity and were referred "penitent cases" by their colleagues far and wide. For example, Rabbi Dov Baer of Lubavitch wrote several special *teshuvah* (repentence) compendia for hasidim in different circumstances.

On this vital subject, Hasidic leaders taught that true *teshuvah* includes both lower and higher dimensions, that it is not enough to merely express remorse for the past and accept the need for self-discipline. Therefore, they recommended specific reparative acts according to each person's outlook and lifestyle. The rebbe usually delighted in teaching his new hasid ways of divine service beyond those of simple atonement.

For instance, in his seminal volume, *Tanya*, Rabbi Schneur Zalman addressed such questions as how to meditate properly and thereby draw closer to the divine. In his preface to this provocative work, he related that many hasidim had explicitly sought such guidance from him. During the heyday of Hasidism, an entire literature for the penitent arose, paralleling and at times surpassing in sophistication such writings in other spiritual traditions.

In their quest for inner attainment, many villagers also implored their rebbe's aid in matters pertaining to the World to Come. A man who dreamed of his parents' suffering in the afterlife might entreat the rebbe to help them on the psychic plane. A woman who dreamed that she had been removed to the other life might approach the rebbe for assistance in avoiding, or delaying, the celestial summons. Hasidim would ask their rebbe's guidance too in choosing names for their newborn children, in order to placate demands from the World to Come.

Indeed, no hasid would dare to act in relation to the departed without the intimate advice of the rebbe. To have sinned against God or a living person, one could make reparations with some ease. But once the other was deceased, the hasid viewed his mentor as indispensable. Nor did death itself terminate this mutually holy relationship: if a hasid died during his rebbe's lifetime, their involvement continued through the latter's devoted prayers.

In short, in virtually all aspects of life, *shtetl* folk turned to the rebbe for inspiration and comfort. Sickness and health, livelihood and commerce, prayer and sacred study, even dealings with the departed—all were part of the rebbe's unique mission to the Jewish people.

AN ARRAY OF HOLY MASTERS

During the beginning years of Hasidism, the term "rebbe" and the individual Hasidic leader who resided in a particular locale were synonymous. As the message of the Baal Shem Tov attracted more and more adherents, many towns and villages produced especially gifted teachers of the Hasidic way. Some, like the Maggid of Mezritch, became renowned for their ascetic, intellectual, and scholastic prowess. Others, like Rabbi Nachman of Bratslav, great-grandson of the Besht, became famous for their fiery insistence on the new path to holiness. Still others, like Wolfe of Zbarazh were widely known for their gentleness and humility. Consequently, the specific personalities and "professional" styles of the Besht's disciples generated popular images of what a rebbe should be like.

Later, as the Hasidic movement continued to expand, the nature of the rebbe's role began to shift. No single figure could successfully minister to thousands in need; and, perhaps equally significant, many communities began to yield more than one Hasidic master. Therefore, somewhat inevitably, diversification among rebbes gradually occurred. People sought counselors and advisors for the particular function in which they excelled: whether it was Talmudic-legalistic skill, healing ability, or Kabbalistic power. In other words, specialization eventually took place.

Community Judges and Eminent Scholars

All the revolutionary power of Hasidism did not dislodge the simple faith of *shtetl* Jews in their major purveyors of the Torah. That is, before the Besht and his adherents came on the scene, each community boasted its own particularly sagacious judge or *rav*. Though some Hasidic leaders wished to transcend this popular institution—which they viewed as overly narrow and legalistic in focus—others, like Rabbi Schneur Zalman, felt the position worth maintaining. They did not want to see true scholars of the Torah denigrated in the eyes of the simple folk: to do so would have been contrary to the basic purpose of Hasidism.

Thus, rather than weaken the institution of the *rav*, many Hasidic rebbes simply adopted the title and some of its related duties. Rabbi Jacob Joseph of Polnoye served as a model for the Hasidic *rav*, as did Rabbi Levi Yitzchok and Rabbi Schneur Zalman, who was given the epithet *"Rav."*

As *rav*, the Hasidic rebbe enjoyed his established authority in the community on the basis of the age-old Talmudic hierarchy. For in the popular view, the *rav* not only decided the law on earth but also for the heavenly realms. Villagers felt they could come to the *rav* for a judgment and summon even the Deity to appear. Sought more for his rabbinical decree than for his secret power or blessing, the *rav* was venerated for his wisdom. Both God and humanity had to abide by his binding *halachic* ("legal") ruling.

For East European Jews, a related though not identical figure of guidance was the *gaon* ("great scholar"). Unlike the *rav*, who was empowered to decide on matters of life and death, sacred and profane, the *gaon* was the pure, not applied, researcher of Torah. His strength flowed from his total immersion in its infinite mysteries; he was regarded as Torah itself. To pious Jews, the *gaon*'s scholarly pursuits were sensed as a fragrance to God; if not for his existence, the universe would instantly cease. His merits were seen as immense.

For this reason, villagers approached him for assistance. In fact, among nonhasidim, the *gaon* was one of the few available to help ordinary folk. The scholarly Rabbi Ezekial Landau was no friend of Hasidism; yet even hasidim would tell how he aided supplicants through the power of his holy study. Such tales were told too of the Vilnaer *Gaon*, the major Hasidic opponent. Some Hasidic rebbes also served in the capacity of *gaon*.

Generally, *gaon* and supplicant shared little intimacy or communication. In the scholar's single-minded inquiry into the lofty, pure realms of Torah, he had nothing concrete to offer: no magic spells, no judgments, no advice. To be rid of the man or woman—the sooner the better—would make for an increase in merit through the *gaon*'s resumed studies. Nevertheless, the scholar might later tell of the increased Torah insight he had been granted from above, as reward for his concern and compassion.

The Good Jew

In the impoverished towns and villages of Eastern Europe, popular Yiddish adages attested to the difficulty of being a Jew; but one who succeeded in becoming a "Good Jew" was considered truly favored by God. At their local synagogues, unlearned folk could hear at public lectures about the ancient heroes of Israel who were the prototype of the Good Jew. If those in days of old could pray for rain, or intercede for others, then one's contemporaries could surely do likewise, many earnestly believed. Even the man or woman who had sinned and repented could act mightily, for "On the place where the penitent stood, not even the most righteous could abide." For example, multitudes flocked to the counsel of

Rabbi Berishl of Krakow—formerly a debauched student who had turned penitent after hearing a Hasidic song.

The Hasidic leaders characteristically welcomed such spontaneous adulation of local Jewish heros, some of whom served in ordinary occupations like bricklaying. Rebbes regarded such people as paragons for the masses and therefore worth emulating closely. Fantastic tales of how Rabbi Leib Sures had threatened the Austrian Emporer were not too wild for the villagers' imagination; they believed that for great virtue, nothing was too marvelous a reward. Indeed, such figures were much easier to celebrate in song and story than reclusive scholars and esoteric savants.

Thus, the Hasidic founders emphasized tales that extolled the Good Jew as a person to be followed. They described him as an exemplar of faith in God, one who refused even to allow money to accumulate in his home overnight: for if he believed that God would bless one anew each day, what was the sense of storing personal savings when others needed immediate funds? Regardless of his own situation, the Good Jew was said to freely offer charity and perform acts of great kindness.

Several Hasidic dynasties, including the Chernobiler and Ruzhiner, eventually established themselves on this model of the Good Jew. They stressed study and prayer less than the harmonious balance of charitable actions and synagogue activities. Furthermore, they downplayed the rebbe's miracle-worker abilities, for such paranormal talents were viewed as an implicit by-product of his holy way of life.

Seers and Healers

Just as the Good Jew emerged from the ancient helping tradition, the Seer came out of the prophetic mode. Perhaps the most famous rebbes in this role were the Seer of Lublin and his disciple, the Ziditchoiver. These figures were renowned for their capabilities to clairvoyantly diagnose or

"read" the soul-auras of others. It is said that the Seer of
Lublin sought as a young man to eliminate his psychic gifts,
for these kept him from his own study, prayer, and contemplation. Later, under the tutelage of older Hasidic masters,
he learned to apply such talents to the service of God.

Shtetl folk often journeyed hundreds of miles, under quite
dangerous circumstances, to attain revelations through mystical "readings"—designed to shed light on one's particular
purpose in life. The Seer of Lublin was credited with the
ability to penetrate beyond time and space, to examine past
lives; on this basis, he would offer his counsel. On other
occasions, we are told, when someone asked the Lubliner for
advice concerning a wedding match, he would look—psychically—to see the bride or groom, and thereupon, offer his
guidance.

Hasidim explained such extraordinary phenomena in the
following way: on the first of day of Creation, the Holy One
fashioned a special light. But when Adam sinned, this sacred
light was withdrawn from the physical realm; only the most
pious could rely on it, to thereby "see from one end of the
universe to the other." Others were said to be given a glimpse
at the hour of their death of that great, white light.

The Baal Shem Tov, the basic model for all rebbes, kept a
volume of the *Zohar* on his desk. Whenever he needed higher
discernment, "he would look into the *Zohar* and see." In this
same vein, the Ruzhiner rebbe would say to the supplicant,
"Let us recite a few chapters of the Psalms and our sight will
be clear. Then, we shall see." Such stories were the mainstay
of Hasidic trust in the rebbe's clairvoyant prowess.

Relatedly, the East European Jewish villagers often revered the rebbe as a miraculous healer. Some rebbes took to
this venerated role as a result of their day-to-day pastoral
work; others, fewer in number, became rebbes having first
experienced popular success as spiritual healers. They recognized that true well-being always involves the whole person.
The Besht himself was extolled for his esoteric knowledge of
health and disease; he regularly prescribed herbal remedies,

laying-on-of-hands, and various mystical rituals to effect his startling cures.

The Talmudic sages had generally viewed the causes of sickness in ethical terms: health is the reward for a proper way-of-life; illness is punishment. Thus, to be "healed" means to be reconciled with the transcendent—and, in Hasidic times, the rebbe was seen as the instrument of this reconciliation. He tended to see disease as ultimately self-inflicted; the supplicant needed to be healed not only of his visible symptoms, but also of the cause of his distress—namely, false or limited consciousness.

Consequently, complete healing was deemed dependent on true penitence or *teshuvah* on the supplicant's part. Hasidim considered the Biblical injunction, "I shall heal them from their savagery," as indicative of healing through *teshuvah*. In the Biblical tale told to demonstrate this concept, Na'aman, the Syrian general, was restored to well-being when he followed the counsel of Elisha. Na'aman pleaded that while he might not be able to break totally from his idolatrous past, he would vow never to stray from his commitment to the God of Israel. Similarly, Menasse the king was healed when he repented of his former path.

Interestingly, certain rebbes referred their followers to specific physicians for treatment. However, rebbes conducted their own diagnoses; they utilized physicians for therapy only and *not* for purposes of diagnosis or prognosis for recovery. Such matters were seen to flow from spiritual forces best left to the rebbe's own power of discernment.

Kabbalists and Miracle Workers

In early Hasidism, every great rebbe was esteemed as a sacred source of mystical insight and strength. In both public discourses—usually conducted on the Sabbath—and in private, *yehidut* sessions, Hasidic masters would reveal some of their secret knowledge of the cosmos and its infinite mysteries. In keeping with traditional Jewish dicta and common sense, they limited their provocative presentations according to the capacity of the listener. However, though practicing Kabbalists had existed for many centuries, the Hasidic leaders transformed what had often become merely an arcane verbal game into the realities of spiritual ecstasy. They sought to induce mystical experiences in their disciples by means of *devekut* ("attunement"), *hitlahavut* ("fervor"), and other altered states of consciousness. They did not simply lecture about highly abstract, symbolic subjects, and not take it further. Some rebbes insisted that personal verification is the key to inner advancement; they decisively repudiated the dry, distant, sometimes ponderous approach of the *Mitnaggedim* toward the celestial secrets.

In an archetypal tale, the great Maggid of Mezritch once came to the Besht to see if he was truly a saint. The Hasidic founder asked him to interpret a particular passage in the *Zohar* and the Maggid of Mezritch did so. Thereupon, the Besht expounded upon the same section and the room became filled with the light of angelic beings. "Your interpretation was correct," said the Besht, "but your way of studying lacked soul." The Maggid immediately became an ardent disciple of his. And, when he assumed the mantle of the Besht's leadership, he too emphasized the experiential implications of the Kabbalah rather than its metaphysical aspects.

As part of his mystical repertory, the Hasidic rebbe was extolled for his ability to create paranormal "signs" or *moftim*. These were associated with the "practical" element of the Kabbalistic system and typically involved complex permutations of the Hebrew alphabet. The Baal Shem Tov was credited with the capacity to make miracles using such esoteric techniques; Rabbi Ber of Radoshitz based his entire ministry on *moftim*, declaring that it was his special task to utilize these in the "greater sanctification of His Name." Such signs usually included demonstrations of mind-over-matter, physical materializations, and uncanny coincidences.

For instance,

> When a hasid came one morning to Rabbi Israel of Vishnitz for
> his regular visit, the rebbe surprised him by asking him to
> davven minhah (to pray the afternoon prayer). Since the visit
> was made in the morning, the hasid, a simple householder,
> was surprised by the rebbe's request, and expressed his sur-
> prise to the rebbe. The rebbe then said, "Never mind. Tell me
> about your business affairs." Again the hasid was surprised
> that the rebbe would withdraw his request in this manner,
> particularly since the rebbe knew all about his business affairs.
> Nevertheless, after some urging by the rebbe, he recounted for
> him a typical day. He ended his account by saying that in the
> evening when he went home, he recited the evening prayer
> twice. When the rebbe questioned him about this, he admitted
> that since his lumber business made it necessary for him to be
> out in the forest during the day, he neglected the afternoon
> prayer, and, in its stead, recited the evening prayer twice. The
> rebbe then repeated that he must davven the afternoon prayer.
> Only then did the hasid understand the rebbe's previous
> injunction.

Intriguingly, while most rebbes felt competent to call upon
God to perform miraculous "signs," they preferred to restrict
these to rare circumstances. For they preached that, "Only very
great *zaddikim* can effect these without upsetting other levels
in a person's balance." They also admonished their followers
that, "Not everything the Besht could do, may we do."

For one thing, some of the greatest rebbes felt so sure of the
ultimate benefits of the person's problem or pain that they
themselves did not wish to alter his situation to obtain a
superficial solution. Thus, perhaps somewhat paradoxically,
they would refer the supplicant to a less farsighted rebbe,
who might be able to effect the desired change. Moreover, the
hasid's insistence for a miraculous intervention usually revealed that he had little faith in God's unfolding plan. Indeed,
the Hasidic founders declared that people should be ashamed
to ask the rebbe for a *mofet*; his wise counsel, not his *moftim*,
were to be prized.

For instance, in response to a hasid who pressed for reports
of a rebbe's paranormal powers, the master's disciple rebuked
him; "I give you the cream [of the rebbe's teachings] and you

want stories [of signs]!" In fact, the Hasidic leaders emphasized, the most exalted miracle of all is to take a simple
person and make a hasid of him.

Ancestral Merit and the Sacred Graveside

The early hasidim regarded all of the rebbe's acts on their
behalf as a reflection of his accumulated merit. They believed
that for his sake, the world itself had been created and
sustained; his saintliness was enormous. Therefore, his followers reasoned: if the rebbe could help them so greatly
during his lifetime, when limited by bodily constraints, how
much more could he accomplish when liberated from physical bonds? Hasidim knew that Jewish tradition clearly taught
that without the ceaseless intercession of the sages in heaven,
the earth would not exist for even a moment.

Because hasidim viewed the rebbe as continuing his work
in the afterlife, they often venerated his descendents as holy
figures—serving through heredity as his earthly "channels."
For instance, the Baal Shem Tov's grandson, Rabbi Barukh of
Medzyboz, attributed much of his ministry's power to the
Besht's own strength flowing through him. In this manner,
the institution of the holy eynikl ("grandson") came into being
in Eastern Europe. Such a personage did not need to claim
heroic virtue for himself; as his ancestor's living proxy and
recipient of merit, he was respected as a mighty figure.

Not surprisingly, the eynikl was basically quite conservative
in his outlook. Because his entire status rested on his ancestor's
past achievement, the eynikl could assume no responsibility
for initiating new ideas or practices. For this reason, some
descendants of great rebbes, like the Besht's great-grandson
Rabbi Nachman of Bratslav, sought to establish themselves as
independent, original thinkers in their own right.

Many shtetl folk confidently came to the eynikl for aid.
They sensed that he was content to bind their loyalties to the

exalted, ancestral dynasty and would not attempt to challenge them personally. Indeed, to those unwilling to make significant changes in their lives, the *eynikl* was probably a less threatening, if more bland, figure than his renowned ancestor.

The *eynikl's* specific assistance usually took the form of prayers offered at his ancestor's graveside. In arduous and dangerous pilgrimages, hasidim often traveled far for this sort of transcendent intervention. Tales of miraculous cures and visions at such sites sustained their faith in the power of this sacred tradition.

Occasional Helpers

Both the sophisticated and the popular *shtetl* advisor needed to refer to colleagues when the occasion arose. At times, one rebbe would send a hasid to another—perhaps because their communication was poor, or the proper rapport had failed to develop. The rebbe might describe this situation as his inability to "descend" to the hasid's level, or to accept him without judging him. Not wishing to abandon the supplicant, the rebbe would therefore recommend him to a colleague.

Sometimes, too, a hasid might himself seek the occasional guidance of another rebbe, while in no way wishing to sever ties with his own master. Perhaps the hasid was simply traveling in the other rebbe's vicinity, or else had deliberately sought him out for his special expertise. If the hasid did not wish to break relations with his own master, such encounters had to be initiated with great delicacy. Otherwise, the hasid might well find himself banished from his own mentor.

Hasidim generally believed that one who did not follow his own rebbe exclusively showed fickleness of character—and perhaps even a tendency to seek illusory shortcuts in personal growth. The leaders taught that a hasid could never recapture the beginning "honeymoon" between him and his rebbe; perpetual courting, for all its delight, would lead to minimal progress.

On occasion, when the rebbe desired to dislodge a hasid from his habitual attitudes and actions, he was sent to a *mokhiah* ("chastiser" or "admonisher"). This referral was especially necessary when the hasid's moral lapse had become chronic and a "crisis" was needed to render his condition acute once more. Because the hasid might have lived with his weakness for several years—and even adapted to it—he might not have sensed his true plight. It might even seem "normal" to him. Consequently, the goal of the *mokhiah* was to shock the hasid into looking at his life from a suddenly different, transformed perspective.

While carrying out this intriguing role, the "holy brothers," Rabbi Elimelekh and Rabbi Zussya, spent many years in exile from their native communities. They would seek out an individual sinner, and disguisedly obtain lodging with him. Then, at night, they would in bitter tears confess their host's sins to him—until he was moved to personally confess and accept the need for penance. At times, a rebbe would send his hasid on such an errand; by the person's example of living piety, he would stir the sinner to *teshuvah*.

If verbal means were incapable of inducing the "inner crisis" necessary for penitence, a melody often proved effective. The Baal Shem Tov appointed one of his disciples to become a cantor, traveling the countryside and awakening the people's yearnings for a more transcendent life. Sometimes, neither word nor music could provoke the person's "crisis," but dance could. The Kalover rebbe was a specialist in this realm and brought many to an inner awakening.

Moreh Derekh: Teacher of the Way

Of all the many, varied "job descriptions" that celebrated the rebbe's far-reaching activities, this one was clearly their favorite. In fact, the latter-day Rabbi Ahrele Roth explicitly wrote to his disciples, forbidding them to refer to him as anything other than *moreh derek* ("teacher of the Way") in serving the divine. The Besht and his successors regarded the spiritual guidance of their hasidim as the rebbe's most crucial task. The Hasidic founders emphasized that no sacred text, however exalted or inspiring, could equal the impact of a living master on peoples' daily lives.

Although the rebbe's discourses frequently centered on the path of heavenly Love and Awe, such talks served mainly as a backdrop to his more personalized teachings. They also helped to strengthen his followers' community involvement. That is, through private, *yehidut* sessions and specially prepared tracts for specific groups of Jews, the rebbe typically offered his most penetrating prescritions for a holy way-of-life. While some rebbes preferred an intuitive and spontaneous method of directing their flock, others promulgated their counsel in a highly systematic manner.

For example, Rabbi Dov Baer of Lubavitch wrote ten separate works for penitents, each treatise aimed at uplifting a particular type of personality. As Chabad's most prolific author of manuals designed for inner advancement, he poetically described his function as a *moreh derekh*. "I certainly have a duty and an obligation," he wrote, "to explain thoroughly, in full detail, the various matters concerning ... methods of worship in mind and heart, each thing in its place ... so that he who has lost his way may not be confused and confuse others."

Jewish life in Eastern Europe was indeed difficult and at times a sheer struggle to survive. Many people suffered from illness, financial hardship, and despair. But by following the advice of leaders like Rabbi Dov Baer of Lubavitch, each man and woman could become "deeply rooted, tied with an enduring knot, never to be severed" from divine wholeness.

CHAPTER THREE

PATHS TO WISDOM

When Rabbi Mendel of Vitebsk arrived in the Holy Land, he had with him a man who was his personal secretary. One day, the secretary was overwhelmed to hear his master pray, "Dear Lord, how well and clear it is known to you that my secretary is a much holier man than I. By rights, he should be the master and I should be his disciple."

A few minutes later, Rabbi Mendel called his secretary and gave him some menial task to do. The secretary could not keep from voicing his amazement at this double attitude. Thereupon, Rabbi Mendel of Vitebsk said, "Yes, this is true. But, that is the transaction that I must have with God concerning my position and yours. Once I have assumed the role of master, I must follow it through without equivocation."

—Or Yesharim

TO EFFECTIVELY CARRY OUT HIS FUNCTION AS A HEALER and a counselor, the Hasidic rebbe clearly needed to be trained for his work. He could certainly not expect to conduct the complex and innumerable aspects of his day-to-day activities without in-depth preparation. As the Hasidic movement in Eastern Europe grew in influence, its founders recognized the importance of adequate training for those followers who would succeed them as rebbes to the Jewish people.

Unfortunately, though, surviving records as to how the Hasidic sages selected a rebbe-to-be from among their hasidim are few and obscure. Nor have accounts come down to us describing in detail how the disciple was trained; no rebbe even went so far as to fully spell out how he himself was groomed for his position. Therefore, utilizing the fragmentary information available to us, we have reconstructed a tentative, yet fairly factual description of the method of selection, preparation, and evaluation, by which a young man became a spiritual leader.

At the outset, we have highlighted the importance of the postulant's capacity to function as a "Good Jew" in his master's eyes. For the Hasidic founders viewed such a personality as essential to effective *shtetl* counseling. We will also briefly examine the specific attributes which the Kotzk, ascetic, and Chabad schools sought to develop in their disciples. Before this interesting exploration, though, we will first look at the rebbe's own attitude toward his task of "grooming" rebbes-to-be.

Bear in mind that our narrative is a composite or gestalt drawn from the anecdotal material existant. Obviously, we can claim no access to the supernal guidance to which the rebbe alluded in this entire process.

Imagine that, on the basis of the Hasidic method, you were to reinstitute the office of the rebbe. Imagine too that it was your task to find those who would eventually serve as rebbe— and that you would have to develop a suitable training program. How would you proceed?

THE REBBE'S DILEMMA

The rebbe who cherished his opportunity to prepare disciples derived great fulfillment in his work; yet he also faced a

very real conflict. In striving to inculcate knowledge and
inner mastery in his hasidim, he sought evidence for their
increasing prowess. He took genuine pride in their achieve-
ments. Simultaneously, though, their success as postulants
signalled to the rebbe that he was personally no longer quite
so needed.

At the outset of Hasidism, this problem was not as acute as
it later became; the early Hasidic leaders were more intent
on furthering the great cause than on solidifying their own
positions. The movement was lively and exciting, its impetus
strong and immediate. Thus, the new and the untried did not
represent much of a threat in Hasidism's beginning phases.
Indeed, because the movement itself had arisen to overturn
the old structures of *shtetl* life, disciples could commit few
grave errors.

Within a few decades, though, this situation changed
markedly. Initially, the Hasidic foes had been protective of
the past and reacted to innovation with suspicion; eventually,
as they gained more bona fides among the established pious,
the rebbes and their followers shifted that way too. Once this
element of conservatism became ingrained, rebbes could no
longer risk that their ardent apprentices—bursting with new
ideas to revitalize Judaism—take over responsibilities dic-
tated by prudence and circumspection. For they could in
their enthusiasm cause more harm than good.

Consequently, the Hasidic rebbe gradually assumed the
role of a father figure to the masses. He became a guide and
an advisor to those on the inner quest, yet one also to be
feared for his intimacy with the divine. This duality did not
always make for smooth relations, for only when the rebbe
felt secure in his disciple's adherence to tradition could he
permit the younger man to act independently. Sometimes,
this situation was prolonged for years, and inevitably, strains
developed.

The tension between the older rebbe and the postulant had
also an oedipal component to it. Symbolically, the congregation was the "mother" and the rebbe the "father." The
younger rebbe-to-be, in the position of "son," may have seen

himself as leading the congregation more appropriately than the older, "father" rebbe. The postulant's impatience, subliminally noticed by the older man, made for tensions between them.

In some instances, postulants had the boldness to become heads of new Hasidic groups within their rebbes' own lifetime, with relatively amicable feelings on both sides. Such was the case with Rabbi Elimelekh, who began leadership of his group in Galicia, with the blessing of his master, Rabbi Dov Baer of Mezritch. Later, and somewhat reluctantly, Rabbi Elimelekh gave his own blessing to his disciple, the Seer of Lublin, to lead a congregation during the former's lifetime. On other occasions, the separations between postulant and rebbe occurred much less peacefully.

Relatedly, an uneasy ambivalence also existed among hasidim when one of them was chosen to be a rebbe-in-training. Originally, the Hasidic activists all had exalted aspirations and rejoiced in the spiritual accomplishments of a peer. However, as time passed, antagonisms arose when the rebbe lifted one of them out of the peer group for special preparation. As tactfully as possible, the rebbe had to ease the group's sense of rejection, such as by declaring that the individual had been selected due to his "loftier, inborn soul." In this way, the others could save face, and one day, give their allegiance to their former associate as their undisputed leader.

THE GOOD JEW

Among all the healers and counselors in the Hasidic world, the "Good Jew" was the general practitioner. His manner of listening and replying was warm and friendly; more than any other Hasidic helper, he felt himself into his supplicant's position and reacted with compassionate concern. In so doing,

he represented to the hasid the merciful God who is all-knowing
and ever-willing to aid humanity.

In seeking appropriate disciples, the rebbe who modeled
himself as the Good Jew typically attracted those with similar inclinations. He valued persons who could take the risk of
relaxing self-control so that they could empathize with the
feelings of others. In selecting postulants, such a rebbe might—
like the Baal Shem Tov—tell a story of a man or woman in a
bad predicament, to see how the would-be disciple might
react. Could the young man actually feel the person's plight,
or did he concern himself merely with the abstract issues of
the tale?

However, the rebbe expected more from disciples than the
capacity to empathize; they also had to possess certain mental qualities. The Good Jew as counselor was supposed to be
able to recover from his identification with the supplicant
and provide genuine insight; he needed to use both intellect
and intuition in his work. Consequently, the rebbe usually
looked for a more "maternal" rather than "paternal" style of
relating; sternness and strict judgment might well be attitudes for dealing with oneself. But for dealing with others,
compassion and nurturance were indicated.

Because of the importance that empathic communication
played in this approach, such factors as one's pronunciation,
inflection, and local habits in gesture and clothing were evalu-
ated closely. Ethnic compatibility was seen as a key determi-
nant in the selection of the Good Jew as future rebbe.

The postulant's training in this orientation mainly involved
actualizing and exercising his inborn capabilities with deliberateness. The major scene of his activity was liturgical
and celebrative. Above all, the disciple had to learn how to
lead synagogue services, so as to inspire enthusiasm and even
ecstasy in his Hasidim. And, without wavering in his own
"one-pointedness" of mind, he had to be sensitive to what
was taking place around him. This dual awareness was in-
stilled through systematic practice. Rabbi Ahrele Roth clearly
addressed this issue:

> He who leads a congregation in prayer should be shown such a
> way that, singing well and observing the melodic modes, he
> will at the same time lift up his broken heart to the Most High,
> and guard himself from pride. . . . It is possible to pray and to
> lead . . . sitting and chanting in the specific modes, and yet to
> be far from self-consciousness.

The disciple was expected to absorb his master's procedures in everyday life. Within certain constraints, he was
encouraged to innovate and elaborate, such as in composing
new melodies and offering new Torah explications and
variations—derived from teachings of his master or associates.

Though all future rebbes were supposed to be Good Jews to
some extent, the specific preparation for rebbehood varied
according to the particular Hasidic school or group. We will
therefore briefly highlight three of the major, separate approaches from this era: those of Kotzk, the ascetics, and those
of Lubavitch or Chabad (their Kabbalistic abbreviation for our
three highest intellectual faculties).

THE KOTZK SCHOOL

Rather than valuing the charismatic, consoling type of
counselor, the Polish school idealized the person who existed
in a state of "perpetual crisis" before the Almighty. The founder
of this approach was the enigmatic Rabbi Menachem Mendel
of Kotzk (known as "the Kotzker"). In a representative passage,
he vividly described this condition of never-ending urgency:

> He who seeks to be a rebbe must ascend dizzying heights and
> descend to vertiginous depths—all in order to seek the truth.
> He must constantly beat down doors—even if his heart bursts
> and his body disintegrates. Heaven and earth may crumble,
> but he must not give way. A rebbe who is not prepared to
> break his own head and skull, how can he teach others?

Above all, these hasidim prized intense awareness and empathy with extreme sensitivity. They respected individuality as the supreme trait of the sage and his adherents. Instead of conducting their activities with warmth and friendliness, rebbes of the Kotzk school projected the image of "lonely men." And they expected their followers to be "lonely men," too. Thus, when rebbe and hasid communicated with one another, they did so in momentary flashes. The spiritual master of Kotzk was supposed to offer only provocative hints, not elaborate explanations.

Typically, disciples best suited for this method were rather introverted and solitary people, given to constant soul-searching and self-scrutiny. They were bold, intuitive thinkers as opposed to great systematizers. Engaged in violent struggle with their own inner "shadows," they tended to be harsh with themselves and others. For such persons, ethnic compatibility was not critically important in their counseling, for they communicated with a crisis orientation. Rebbes spoke with Talmudic idiom and insight in their terse remarks to supplicants.

To a large extent, to train a disciple for the Kotzk school involved teaching him to "unlearn" what he had previously mastered. The importance of heroes or models was downplayed; the postulant was encouraged to seek for wisdom within his own soul. If he expressed too great an admiration for a sage, the rebbe might rebuke him, "For the sake of a long white beard you are willing to sell your God?" Interestingly, the Biblical paragon for this school was not an Abraham or Moses, but the figure of the Egyptian Pharaoh, who refused to budge in his judgment despite all the plagues God wrought upon him.

The Kotzk disciple was expected to pursue Talmudic study and to hide all "pious" mannerisms that might attract hero-worship from the common folk. When his enthusiasm began to ignite others, he was instructed to contain this fervor and direct it solely to the divine. "We are here to raise heaven higher," was their founder's stern admonition.

In short, the postulant's intense passion was not to be an

enveloping, warming fire, but a narrow and focused, all-consuming white heat. The chief Kotzk dictum was: "God wants the flame on the altar to burn with a small flame." To those seeking training for this unique Hasidic system, the rebbe would snap the questions, From? To? Why? How? He accepted only the most earnest and unadorned stutterings in response. To him, all embellishments and artifice were worthless—tossed back at the speaker with a mocking gesture.

THE ASCETIC HERO

Neither parental indulgence nor crisis were the forte of the ascetic hero. Such a rebbe concentrated on control and power. Known as "the mighty man who subdues his inclination" through sacred service, he prized severe self-denial as the means to potency in heaven and on earth. The greater our self-control, the larger our strength, the ascetics taught. Instead of emphasizing natural warmth or intellectual prowess, these rebbes extolled the virtues of self-restraint. They expected their disciples to become adept in abstinence and self-possession at all times.

With this particular outlook, such rebbes examined with great scrutiny the day-to-day actions of their postulants. By focusing on apparently mundane, trivial behavior, these spiritual teachers sought to develop in their followers a tremendous inner might, unshakable through all of life's adversities. They were instructed how to awaken and master their senses, and how to transform them into holy functions. And, hasidim who trained for this approach learned to disregard utterly their lesser impulses for immediate gratification.

Some of the provocative advice of such rabbis as Reb Ahrele Roth has come down to us:

The foundation of all [inner] effort is that it makes no difference whether one feels up or down. One must be like a wood-
chopper working for his wages ... who does not care if it is
summer or winter, cold or warm; he always does what he has
to do.

One should never say, "I am not with it today." I tell you here,
in this holy place, that if anyone ever again during his life says,
"I am not with it now," he is not my disciple. . . . To my
disciple, this phrase does not apply.

Rabbi Elimelekh of Lizensk, the ascetic hero who bathed in
icy water, rolled naked in the snow, and sat on ant hills,
expounded on learning self-discipline in the following manner:

When you are free at any time ... especially when you are
sitting alone in a room without doing anything ... you must
create in your soul the image ... of a great and fierce fire
burning before you, its flames reaching the heart of heaven.
And you, for the sake of sanctifying His Blessed Name, break
the hold of your desire, and cast yourself into that very fire.

and to quote him further:

When reading the first sentence of the Sh'ma creed and the
first blessing of the Sh'moneh Esreh, you ought to meditate
as mentioned before. Moreover, you ought to *intend* that
even if all the nations of the world would inflict the greatest
pains on you and skin you alive in order to bring about your
denial of His Blessed Unity, you would much rather suffer all
these pains than, God forbid, accede to them. You ought to
describe this in your knowing and thinking as if they were
actually doing all this to you, as if you experienced it all fully.
It is in this way that you will be able to achieve what you
ought to in the reading of the Sh'ma and the Amidah prayer.
    Even at the time of eating and procreating, you ought to have
the same intention. As soon as you begin to feel sensual pleasure,
visualize and experience this image and then say in your mouth
as well as in your heart that you would have greater joy and
pleasure in the observance of the commandment: "I shall be
sanctified" than from the pleasure you derive from the sensual
enjoyment. This you will say to yourself time and time again.
    As a proof of this, you must get your soul in such readiness
that if they were to grab you in order to murder you in the

midst of your eating or procreating, and would inflict grave pains on you, you would find greater joy in the sanctification of His Blessed Name than this sensual pleasure. Be very careful, however, that these intentions and statements are made in great truth. These things must become engraved in absolute truth upon the tablets of your heart and in its very depth and center. Do not attempt to deceive yourself or the Most High.

In today's terms, the ascetic hero was akin to the mythic dragon-slayer on his pilgrimage toward individuation. The rebbe's method of discourse was basically to instill fortitude in his followers—and consequently, he demanded of them great austerity and deliberateness. The rebbe concentrated his activity in the realms of fasting and frequent prayer and meditation. He attached little importance to ethnic compatibility because such inner power was seen to transcend and supersede ethnic allegiances. In sum, the ascetic rebbe trained his disciples to be "constant holocausts" before God in order to gain merit for their fellow Jews. This reward was deemed granted in the form of tangible blessings.

This emphasis on asceticism, however, was not always appropriate, as can be seen in the following tale of Rabbi Elimelekh withholding his acceptance of the hasid.

For six years and then for another six years, Rabbi David of Lelov had done great penance: he had fasted from one sabbath to the next, and subjected himself to all manner of rigid discipline. But even when the second six years were up, he felt that he had not reached perfection and did not know how to attain what he still lacked. Since he had heard of Rabbi Elimelekh, the healer of souls, he journeyed to him to ask his help. On the evening of the sabbath, he came before the *zaddik* with many others. The master shook hands with everyone except Rabbi David, but from him he turned and did not give him a glance. The rabbi of Lelov was appalled and left. But then he thought it over and decided that the master must have taken him for someone else. So he approached him in the evening, after the prayer, and held out his hand. But he was treated just as before. He wept all night and in the morning resolved not to enter the *zaddik*'s House of Prayer again, but to leave for home at the end of the sabbath. And yet—when the hour of the holy third meal had come, he could not restrain himself and crept up to the window. There he heard the rabbi say:

"Sometimes people come to me who fast and torment themselves, and many a one does penance for six years and then for another six—twelve whole years! And after that, they consider themselves worthy of the holy spirit, and come and ask me to draw it down to them; I am to supply the little they still lack. But the truth of the matter is that all their discipline and all their pains are less than a drop in the sea, and what's more: all that service of theirs does not rise to God, but to the idol of their pride. Such people must turn to God by turning utterly from all they have been doing, and begin to serve from the bottom up and with a truthful heart."

When Rabbi David heard these words, the spirit moved him with such force, that he almost lost consciousness. Trembling and sobbing, he stood at the window. When the Havdalah was concluded, he went to the door with faltering breath, opened it in great fear, and waited on the threshold. Rabbi Elimolekh rose from his chair, ran up to his motionless visitor, embraced him and said: "Blessed be he that comes!" Then he drew him toward the table and seated him at his side. But now Eleazar, the *zaddik*'s son, could no longer restrain his amazement.

"Father," he said, "why, that is the man you turned away twice because you could not endure the mere sight of him!"

"No, indeed!" Rabbi Elimelekh answered. "That was an entirely different person! Don't you see that this is our dear Rabbi David!"

THE CHABAD LEADER

To an extent, the Chabad or Lubavitch rebbe was expected to blend all three of the preceding types within his personality; yet, he was also supposed to systematically promulgate the sophisticated philosophy of Rabbi Schneur Zalman, the group's founder. For, according to him, "A rebbe's task is to teach Hasidism according to the spirit of the times and the needs of the people." Therefore, the Lubavitch rebbe sought the sort of disciple who would record his discourses "as he says them and as he means them." Lubavitch Hasidism cherished verbal and conceptual abilities and prized the correct pronunciation of the White Russian dialect of their leaders.

Chabad rebbes directed their greatest efforts to those whom they considered the proper "psychic mind-and-heart stuff for the doctrine and its acts." They strove to train persons who "see each thing with a pure clarity, even things which at first cause the heart to become enflamed ... and who have the ability to remove the heart's excitement and inspect ... with the mind's eye." Along with such lofty discernment, one had to develop also a lively and active imagination. Thus, the results of his inner work could be translated into daily life. As the term *chabad* suggested, one's mythic existence was to move between the poles of the *wise* child and the old *sage*.

The preparation of the Lubavitch rebbe-to-be was multi-faceted. It encompassed such specific activities as absorbing all previous *chabad* doctrines, participating in didactic elaborations between rebbe and his disciples, and acquiring an immense repertory of Hasidic stories to be used as concrete illustrations for the often highly abstract teachings. The *farberengen*, or group celebrations, were the major arenas in the young man's training. Intriguingly, while the postulant had little freedom in the matter of *ma'amarim* or public discourses, he was allowed greater automony in the relams of song and informal talks (*sihot*)—for these involvements were also esteemed as gateways to the divine. Like the other Hasidic schools, Lubavitch endeavored to prepare the rebbe-to-be for many varied situations.

APPRENTICESHIP FOR SACRED WORK

The rebbe's position was not a simple one. He had to be many things to many different people. Heart and mind, soul and intellect—all had to skillfully blend in day-to-day life. A wrong word could literally plunge a Hasid into despair or foolish recklessness. For this reason, the rebbe sought a comprehensive training—rigorous and yet gentle—for his disciple, to prepare him for spiritual mastery. While differences in emphasis existed among the various Hasidic groups, the rebbe typically urged the hasid to be involved in the study of both written and oral Torah. He observed the hasid's behavior in different life situations, and supervised his prayer life, involving many counseling sessions.

First, the rebbe directed with keen attention his postulant's intellectual pursuits. He ordinarily instructed the young man in what to read and also gave him special, esoteric volumes of material not accessible to most Jews. Some rebbes kept certain Kabbalistic texts for their chosen followers; for the information was felt to be quite dangerous in the hands of the untutored.

For example, Rabbi Schneur Zalman, the Lubavitch founder, possessed in his private library several works that were strictly forbidden even to his inner circle. These sacred texts were marked "Under Rabbi Gershom's ban in this world and the next." Rabbi Schneur Zalman's own son dared not read them. Once, a fire destroyed a considerable portion of this library and the Lubavitch leader asked his son if he recalled anything from these lofty books so that he might stimulate his father's failing memory. His son replied that he had certainly not violated the ban to read them. Thereupon, the sage rebuked him, "For Hasidic wisdom, one should risk even his life in the World to Come."

In another interesting anecdote, we are told that the Baal Shem Tov as a young man was given access to the secret writings of Rabbi Adam Besht, a mysterious holy figure. So significant was this event in the Hasidic founder's life that it became the subject of numerous legends about him.

Typically, the rebbe examined his disciple' progress in reading and clarified difficult passages for him. In this regard, Lubavitch Hasidism introduced an intriguing reward for successful completion of a course of study: the rebbe would interpret a seemingly mundane Torah section in a manner that revealed its hidden, mystical insights.

Besides such training through Kabbalistic texts, Hasidic discipleship incorporated oral instruction, both group and individual. Usually, the postulant would intensely study his lessons before reviewing them with the rebbe, who thereupon offered corrections and further explanations. The rebbe also encouraged his colleagues to repeat to the rebbe-to-be various discourses they had presented before his birth or during his childhood. In such cases, they also communicated the mood and context of their earlier talks, not simply the intellectual content. In this way, the rebbe-to-be might experience the entire scene as though he had personally attended.

Though both book and oral learning were emphasized as central to the disciple's development, the Hasidic leaders clearly preferred the spoken word. They felt that such lessons conveyed far more than writing—as oral methods included subtle but essential nuances, inflections, gestures, and bodily cues. Moreover, these discourses brought greater emotional intimacy to the relationship; and thus, rebbe and hasid especially prized such discussions.

In addition, the very fact of the rebbe's presentation was itself a measure of the esteem in which he held his hasid. The rebbe never wasted a lecture on those not a ready receptacle to comprehend it; indeed, to do so was likened to masturbation. Thus, knowing the high value that the rebbe placed on his

speeches, the postulant was doubly motivated when he received one.

Yet, because the rebbe's duties entailed far more than aca-
demic knowledge, he could not rely merely on verbal training
for his hasidim. He was not simply a scholar, but a counselor
and a healer as well. As a leader of many Jews, he spent his
days reflecting a spectrum of spontaneous actions that were
significant and holy. These could not be overtly taught; the
disciple had to observe his master directly.

Consequently, in a famous Hasidic anecdote, Rabbi Leib
Sures was asked why he had journeyed from afar to apprentice himself with a particular mentor. "I have come to see
how he ties his shoelaces," he replied. However, not every
slightest act the rebbe committed was held to "unleash hidden worlds"—the postulant needed to learn how to distin-
guish the mundane from the apparently mundane, the inci-
dental from the truly important. For the rebbe was indeed
regarded as a "supernal mirror," a reflection of the divine. As
one hasid remarked when his master died, "I had the feeling
that he was the Infinite in a physical body." This was no idle
statement, but one which resulted from firsthand witnessing
of his rebbe's life.

For this reason, close observation of the master was essential to each disciple's training. Every word and deed was
examined at close range; often, great meaning was found
hidden in apparently commonplace statements or gestures.
Rabbi Zvi Elimelekh tersely related, "When my grandfather
served his rebbe, the hasidim watched his every move."
Nevertheless, hasidim were never encouraged to imitate or
mimic their rebbe. To the hasid who expected the Lekho-
witcher rebbe to be "just like his father," his son pointedly
replied, "I *am* just like my father. He never aped anyone.
Neither do I."

The rebbe's position rested also on his work in prayer,
intercession and liturgy, on deeds of kindness and counseling.
As a result, the rebbe-to-be was expected to attain proficiency
in all of these activities. Typically, the *yehidut* was the time
set aside for such tutoring; the rebbe would allocate special

tasks to be accomplished and periodically ask for a progress report or update. To encourage greater autonomy on the disciple's part, the rebbe sometimes performed for him acts of great warmth and favor. Such surprise visits helped instill in the postulant stronger self-confidence in his work.

Also, the rebbe supervised his disciples' *yehidut* sessions with individual hasidim; he wished to see how his postulants advised others in need. The rebbe often supplemented such "practicum" work with esoteric teachings, such as on the secret aspects of "soul-reading" and healing. For instance, the Lubavitcher Rabbi Dov Baer Schneori declared that from his father he had learned:

> On the level where the soul stands in the primeval thought [of God] all the details of its work here below are included— whether it is to be active or passive, though in either mode souls receive passively from those above them, and in turn actively influence those below them.... The proper way to look at a Jew is to see him as he stands in the primeval thought [of the divine].

This mystical feature of the *yehidut* was central to the rebbe's function as a true healer. He was ascribed the ability to make use of a variety of paranormal powers that normally lie dormant within each soul, in order to help the supplicant. Such capabilities were said to include clairvoyance, telepathy, and the ability to foretell the future. The most advanced sages were venerated for their capacity to communicate with ascended saints, angels and other celestial beings. Thus, as part of his general training program, the rebbe typically sought to awaken these powers in his disciple. The permutation of Hebrew letters to form sacred names of God was a key Kabbalistic technique but there were others, also secret in nature. When the rebbe revealed these "names" for his postulant's final "unification" exercise, his training was over.

We are told, though, that such exotic realms require great inner preparation. The Baal Shem Tov once tested Rabbi Gershon Kittover to see if he could assist in the uplifting of departed souls. Following his master's meditative instructions,

Rabbi Gershon uttered the appropriate Kabbalistic prayers. Suddenly, he was faced with the onrush of countless souls coming to be helped, and he fainted. The Besht had to intervene. Hasidic adherents often recounted tales of how their rebbe "mended" souls at night. To be allowed to watch such exalted proceedings was considered an unusual privilege and honor.

Generally, though, the Hasidic leaders themselves minimized the importance of exercising paranormal powers for their own sake. They viewed these as always subordinate to specific spiritual goals and insisted that their disciples be careful with such explosive matters. As one rebbe aptly remarked, "I can make you into a 'seer' in half an hour. So what?" To prove himself worthy, the postulant had to show ethical sensitivity and wisdom in approaching the extrasensory world as well as the mundane.

Often, the rebbe supervised the rebbe-to-be in the task of answering his correspondence from those seeking advice. Serving as his father's secretary, Rabbi Joseph Isaac Schneersohn responded to such letters; later, his father inspected and critiqued these. When he was satisfied with his son's work in this capacity, he entrusted him with counseling *yeshiva* students, and still later, with the school's administrative functions. In making these appointments, his father delegated growing responsbility to him.

As part of his teaching, the rebbe frequently posed existential problems to his postulants and weighed their answers. In an illustrative example, the Kotzker once called two of his disciples into his study and stated, "I have two questions before me. One concerns a woman in difficult labor; the second, a man mortally ill. If I pray for one, the other must die. Who shall I pray for?"

Ashamed to speak, one disciple kept silent, thinking, "If the rebbe himself doesn't know, how can I?"

But Rabbi Wolfe Strikover, the other disciple, spoke up and replied, "Pray for the man's recovery. Heaven has enough souls to send down, so that you can also pray for the mother and her child."

The Kotzker was delighted with this answer and said, "You have opened a door for me and invigorated me."

Sometimes, the rebbe even shared his depression with his trainee, for such moods were almost inevitable in *yehidut* activity. These had to be faced and experienced. Thus, the great Seer of Lublin, renowned for his paranormal powers, once confided to Rabbi Moshe of Sambor, "People come to me in a depression and they leave with glowing faces. And I, I remain in a depression, in a darkness without light." To properly take on such heavy duties, the rebbe-to-be had to be exposed to the thorns as well as the roses in his path.

INNER TESTS

Despite such emotional strains, rebbes derived great benefit from their exalted position within the *shtetl* world. They held tremendous status and prestige among hasidim; their reputation sometimes extended thousands of miles, to Jews on distant continents. People in every walk of life came to them for advice on even the most intimate matters. It is no wonder that many sought this role, without understanding its corresponding pains or hardships. Therefore, the rebbe had to constantly test his disciple's motivation, to make sure that he still pursued lofty goals—not those of fame, pride, or fortune. Such tests were often quite ingenious, for the rebbe at times placed many impediments in his postulant's path. In this context, and perhaps a larger one, Rabbi Nachman of Bratslav aptly observed, "God is hidden in the obstacle. The wise man knows this; the fool turns back."

Just as there was no single method to train disciples, there was no sole technique to test their inner commitment. Some rebbes put much emphasis on the use of tests; others viewed deliberate challenges as only of minor significance. Still others dispensed with tests entirely. Of course, the approach varied too with the postulant's specific personality. Each rebbe had his own unique style. Nevertheless, such assessments generally fulfilled a dual purpose: those who lacked a true "calling" were rejected, and more importantly, the testing strengthened the will of those who had been truly "called" to leadership.

Rabbi Elimelekh, who followed the model of the ascetic hero, severely tested those who wished to become his disciples. Periodically, he refused to even acknowledge them; he would wait for them to appear again and again, braving his apparent wrath. Only after the hasid had proven his determination by repeatedly seeking the master's presence would he relent and take him under his wing. Rabbi Elimelekh once tested Rabbi Naftali of Ropshitz by rejecting him with the caustic comment, "I don't want any thoroughbreds." Later, after seeing the younger man's determination, Rabbi Elimelekh accepted him as a rebbe-to-be.

Interestingly, the Hasidic founders frequently used verbal barbs (bitush) and counterbarbs as tools to sharpen true vocation. The Yiddish language itself is filled with such aphorisms. Sometimes, the rebbe or an older hasid would expose a disciple in this way to measure his egoism.

Hasidic tradition tells an interesting story on this theme. Once, during his father's incumbency, Rabbi Dov Baer of Lubavitch went to visit a small town. Still in his teens, there he found an older Hasid whose method of praying displeased him. When Rabbi Dov Baer expressed his disapproval, the old man grabbed him by the lapels and shook him furiously. "What did your father have in mind when he sired you!" he exclaimed. "How can you expect me to pray in your manner? You haven't even begun to serve God!"

Later, the old man visited Rabbi Schneur Zalman, his master and Rabbi Dov Baer's father. The father warmly greeted the elder and said, "I want to thank you. You have made my son into a hasid!"

There are a variety of stories describing the tests that the early rebbes utilized. The Lubliner considered the greatest measure to be a temptation successfully overcome; Rabbi Uri felt that a hasid's patience had to be sorely tried before leading others. Rabbi Moshe Leib of Sassove would ask postulants whether they had yet reached even the lowest rung in "the love of Israel"; he pointed out that if they had, they should literally be able to suck the pus out of the wound of a fellow Jew. Perhaps less dramatically, each Lublin disciple had to tell a tale about the city without once mentioning its name.

Sometimes, rebbes required prolonged personal and menial service as proof of the hasid's inner worth; they viewed such tasks as indicative of his humility and diligence. Thus, Rabbi Zvi of Rymanov demonstrated his readiness for rebbehood in the way in which he daily made his master's bed. In other instances, virtually heroic acts of selflessness were expected. Rabbi Nachman of Bratslav often sent his disciple, Rabbi Nathan, on long journeys to carry out certain inexplicable, seemingly trivial acts. One hasid so yearned to attend Rabbi Barukh of Medzyboz's discourses that the former was prepared to die while listening. Rabbi Mendel of Kotzk even demanded of one of his disciples and close friends that he burn his writings on the Talmud.

One set of assessments typically involved acquired knowledge and wisdom. Usually, the master sought a certain mental agility in his disciples—not simply Talmudic scholarship or cleverness, as the Hasidic opponents favored, but rather a kind of inner proficiency that enabled the hasid to deal with the Torah as the mind of God. In our own idiom, if the rebbe felt that the younger man managed to make the right mythic moves with the text, he was then fully accepted.

Another key test was to observe how the postulant made use of the teachings he received: could he successfully integrate these into his day-to-day life? Did any of his actions betray the expectation that his wisdom would increase as a result of his studies? Or, was he simply inflexible and overly rigid in applying what he had learned? Such questions had to be decisively answered before the disciple could be wholly embraced; either the rebbe himself or a mature appointee usually conducted these observations.

Similarly, the rebbe scrutinized the kind of counseling issues his postulant raised or the answers he gave to problems, which resembled modern role-playing exercises. "A woman came to see me and she asked . . ." the rebbe would recount. "Show me what you would have done." Such questions were truly revealing. Did the young man understand the real, underlying matters, or was he misled by surface features? The rebbe also had to determine whether the disciple was too squeamish or too moralistic—and therefore unable to help people with certain painful problems. Occasionally, the rebbe contrived a meeting for the postulant with a person mired in an especially unsavory situation—to see how the disciple would react. For, the Hasidic founders emphasized, "to rescue a man in quicksand, you must be willing to step into the mud."

Not all rebbes, though, tested their disciples. Some rebbes were more eager than others for them and accepted whomever showed a genuine interest. The renowned Maggid of Mezritch, like his mentor, the Besht, welcomed all comers; however, the Maggid did so in a rather formal manner. Rabbi Schneur Zalman similarly took in all who flocked to him. Yet, he once challenged his own grandson, Rabbi Nahum.

In this interesting anecdote, the young man was preparing for his wedding. He proudly put on his new fur coat, whereupon his grandfather asked to make a rip in it. Upon his grandson's adamant refusal, the sage said to him with disdain, "You won't amount to much." As the Lubavitch founder had predicted, his grandson failed to become a rebbe when his father died.

Some rebbes, like the Seer of Lublin, would not accept a disciple unless he first spent some time studying with him. The Seer's enclave resembled a "finishing school" for rebbes-to-be; nearly all the rebbes of Hungary, Galicia, and Poland had some training at this house of study. However, it seems clear that the Seer of Lublin did not so much intellectually shape his postulant as offer himself as a day-to-day model. The Seer, like the other great rebbes, had to be sure that the disciple was indeed ready to assume such great responsibilities. His achievement of this long sought goal was a matter of much rejoicing.

DYNASTIC TRAINEES

As we have mentioned earlier, the Hasidic movement gradually gave rise to various spiritual dynasties. These were based on the bloodlines of their founders or initial leaders. The dynastic trainee was under even more severe scrutiny than his nondynastic counterpart, though the testing assumed different forms.

In cases where the rebbe was born to his office, it was taken for granted that his father and mother had made the act of conception a conscious and deliberate one. "These are the generations of Isaac, son of Abraham. Abraham begat Isaac." In interpreting this apparent redundancy, one rebbe explained that Abraham deliberately begat Isaac as his opposite, for this was God's will.

During the mother's pregnancy, the Hasidic community expressed a watchful concern for her experiences. The parents were sanctified and encouraged in acts of heroic charity; this procedure followed the Biblical pattern exemplified in the tales of Samson and Samuel. At birth, the Hasidic rebbe-to-be was wrapped in a special swaddling cloth. His weaning, first haircut, learning of the Hebrew alphabet—all were deemed matters of marked ceremony and interest. Later, the rebbe even atoned for the possible hurt he had inflicted on his mother while she had nursed him as an infant. Not surprisingly, teachers for the young rebbe-to-be were chosen with particular care. The father-rebbe took special pains to teach his son privately and instruct him in counseling methods.

It is obvious, therefore, that a dynastic crown prince could not escape the awareness of his sacred vocation. The little rebbe-to-be knew what he was and what he was to become. We are told that in his youth, Rabbi Israel, the son of the

Maggid of Chortkov, was once engaged in a Talmudic debate with a visiting scholar. Having proven his skill, the lad was scolded by his father, who explained that the Torah had not been given so that one could show off.

Often, the young rebbe-to-be retorted hotly to such reproof. Rabbi Naftali of Ropshitz once asked his son Rabbi Eliezer, the future Rebbe of Dzhikov, "How is it that you let yourself be guided by the *yezer hara* ("evil urge")? Could you not learn from him?" continued the father. "He never weakens—he is always on the job."

"How could I learn from him?" replied young Eliezer. "The evil urge himself has no evil urge!"

The mother of Rabbi Hirsch of Ziditchoiv would check her children when they returned from the synagogue to see whether they had prayed earnestly: she inspected them for signs of perspiration on their faces. Once, she told her oldest son, Rabbi Zvi Hirsh, that she had not found any sweat on him. "Go and see how your younger brothers are sweating," she remarked. "This is a sign that they have prayed in earnest. And you? Like a dry tree."

Rabbi Zvi replied, "Mother, if sweat is a sign of prayer, then a horse is wiser than man. For only the lazy horses sweat when they run. The good horses don't sweat at all."

Young rebbes-to-be possessed a strong sense of their own authenticity. As inner-directed persons, they saw themselves as responsible only to the Almighty. Their colleagues and teachers soon discovered how difficult it was to persuade them to listen to others. "I was an orphan. No one taught me but God," the Ruzhiner was heard to say. "Even before the Messiah I shall not bend, but insist that my teaching is true."

At the age of six, Rabbi Nachman of Bratslav replied with these words to his mother's accusation of religious laxity, "I am truly one who forsakes evil!" At times, this sort of attitude was even directed to heaven. Legend has it that when Rabbi Nachman was not shown any new visions, he wept until heaven relented and he saw.

Rebbes-to-be often hid their spiritual prowess, not only from outsiders, but also from their own family members.

Parents and teachers treated them with great severity. The Szigeter was taken to the river by his father-in-law who trained him. There, his father-in-law chopped a hole in the ice, had him immerse in the river, and, forbidding him to dry himself, instructed him to return to the House of Study. All this was done in the urgency of preparing the Szigeter to lead some day. Rabbi Joshua of Belz told his Hasidim how terrified he was when, in his youth, he understood the full impact and importance of leadership.

Tradition has it that the two sons of Rabbi Shmuel of Lubavitch were once playing the game of rebbe and hasid. Rabbi Zalman Aaron, then seven years old, was playing rebbe while his younger brother, Rabbi Shalom Dov Baer, then five years old, played hasid. The younger one girded his loins with a prayer sash and knocked softly at the door. When asked to enter, he timidly approached his brother and said, "Master, please give me a *tiqun* ("rectification") for my soul."

"What have you done?" the older one demanded.

"I have stolen a pickle from Mother," was the reply.

At this point, Zalman Aaron laughed, whereupon Shalom Dov Baer, in the heat of frustration, turned and said, "You are not a rebbe. A rebbe never laughs at the distress of a hasid."

In another tale, the brothers were playing the same game in the identical manner. The younger one asked for a *tiqun* for not having recited the blessing after eating an apple. Zalman Aaron replied, "For the next forty days you are to recite a blessing out of the prayer manual after eating any food."

"You did not do it right!" Shalom Dov Baer reproached him.

"How can you say this?" Zalman Aaron argued. "I myself watched Daddy through the keyhole when a hasid asked him the same question. I gave you his reply."

"I, too, watched Daddy," said the younger brother. "But you didn't do it right. Daddy always *sighs* before he answers."

This childhood game proved prophetic, for it was Rabbi Shalom Dov Baer who later became rebbe, not his older brother.

THE CORONATION

Having met all his inner tests and achieved his last "unification" within, the rebbe-to-be was now ready for his new position. Typically, the rebbe announced the attainment of this stage both to others and to the young man himself. In speaking of his successful disciple, the rebbe might say, "He is already a Good Jew.... Everything I have, he has." In calling him to the Torah reading on the synagogue podium before the assembled hasidim, the rebbe would read with great intensity, "A prophet like you [Moses] will I raise up." Privately, he would reiterate too his satisfaction with the disciple's accomplishments, for few were fit to take on such serious and sacred work. "Go with your strength and save Israel," the master might say. Or, "I have nothing more to teach you. Go, become a rebbe."

As his final act of training, the rebbe might teach his postulant a paranormal skill previously kept hidden, or publicly bestow upon him a staff and ritual belt. After years of close, daily involvement, the two men had overcome the chasm between them. With his official ordination, the former disciple was considered by his fellow hasidim to have completed his arduous preparation. They regarded him as a true healer in a world yearning for redemption.

Yet, in a way, the new rebbe was just beginning his calling. Despite the help that he could now offer others, he would rightfully insist that he was still learning. From time to time, he would meet with colleagues and confer with them. And he would come to know the twin emotions of joy and sadness when the time came for him to train his own successor. Only then would he fully comprehend what his own rebbe had done for him.

CHAPTER FOUR

YEHIDUT: THE DIVINE ENCOUNTER

When a Jew comes and tells me of his worries, about matters of the body and of livelihood, I listen carefully. His soul tells me of [its] worries and trembling. Therefore, I must give a counsel that will help to solve both the physical and the spiritual problems. The body speaks for itself and the soul speaks for itself. And, he who answers must answer them in their relation to one another.

The secret of life is flow, and everyone has to receive the influx of life in the same way as he has to give of the flow of life. He who does not receive and give at the same time is a fruitless tree.

—Rabbi Hirsch of Ziditchoiv

DESPITE THE BONDS OF COMPASSION that united Jewish family and community life in Eastern Europe, many people at times felt the need for personal guidance and direction. To be sure, religious leaders before the Hasidic rise offered their help to the masses; yet, such aid was rather limited in scope,

mainly encompassing questions of Jewish Law and its interpretation. For instance, a woman might have sought the rabbi's
decision on whether meat she had purchased had been properly slaughtered; her husband might have needed a judgment
on whether his home had been suitably readied for Passover.

Nevertheless, almost inevitably, *shtetl* existence carried with
it many other, day-to-day problems involving livelihood and
finance, sickness and health, marriage and family, and spiritual longings. Few indeed were those never pained by doubt
or uncertainty about their course of their lives; some more
than others desperately yearned for words of comfort or
inspiration. But aside from offering occasional, informal counsel and prayer for the Almighty's assistance, the intellectual
elite had little inclination for more sustained involvement:
the rarefied study of the Torah's mysteries was their highest
aim.

In contrast, with a sense of revolutionary fervor, the Besht
and his disciples declared that *all* aspects of the world are
holy and wait to be redeemed, back to their original Source.
Even such seemingly mundane realms as one's home or place
of business harbor the sacred shards of the Holy One, they
taught. As the Baal Shem Tov remarked, "In everything in
the universe there are Holy Sparks. Nothing is devoid of
these Sparks, not even wood or stones. This is also true of
man's deeds."

Thus, as the Hasidic movement swiftly arose and swept
across the village landscape, its founders developed a particular means—the *yehidut*—to provide inner direction for their
many followers. Through this structured dialogue, rebbes were
able to directly aid hasidim with their personal difficulties,
and thereby restore greater wholeness to their lives. For the
Besht recognized all human concerns as legitimate for spiritual counseling.

Certainly, the Hasidic leaders introduced many opportunities for *shtetl* folk to grow through association with others.
The rebbe and hasid often met in the synagogue or passing
one another on the street; at lively *farbrengens*, hasidim enjoyed a warm comraderie and a sense of belonging. Yet, such

contacts were invariably highly public, or else rather casual encounters; neither party was really prepared to transact at depth. Therefore, the rebbes instituted the separate institution of the *yehidut*, using as their model the Baal Shem Tov's original sessions with fellow Jews seeking guidance.

What especially distinguished the *yehidut* from other relationships in the Hasidic world was its specialized, formal makeup and its relative privacy. The rebbe offered himself as a spiritual counselor and the hasid came to him as one in need of advice; each person's status was clear and distinct. And, while some rebbes required their *gabbai* ("secretary") to be present during the encounter, it was nevertheless an extremely intimate one. No subject was deemed too private for discussion; and yet, this was not simply a confession of one's misdeeds. As the Hasidic tract *Hayom Yom* concisely observed, "The intent of the *yehidut* is to clarify one's position, to define a way of [divine] service . . . and to unite oneself to the rebbe in complete union."

Although such sacred dialogue took place more than two hundred years ago, it would be foolish for us to overlook its very real complexities. Long before the emergence of modern depth psychology with the ideas of Freud, Jung, and Adler, Hasidic sages were well aware of the subtleties involved in guiding the inner development of others. Some hasidim would quite unconsciously, out of guilt or shame, seek to mask their true conflicts. Others might, due to their embarrassment, preface their remarks with the classic disclaimer, "Rebbe, it is my friend who has the following problem."* For such reasons, the hasid's mentor typically relied on an array of diagnostic and therapeutic intuitions to help him penetrate to the real situation. Many decades preceding Freud's pioneering efforts, these methods often reflected sophisticated theories of personality and achieved significant results.

In this chapter and the next, we will therefore focus in

---

*To which one Hasidic sage is said to have replied, "Then, your friend is a fool! For he should have come to speak with me directly and attributed his problem to someone he knew."

depth upon the provocative intricacies of the *yehidut*—particularly the rebbe's varied approaches to uncovering the hasid's disturbance and then dealing with it therapeutically. Having effectively diagnosed the hasid's difficulty, the rebbe was then in a position to offer his *ezah*, or specific directive for action. Before embarking on this intriguing subject, though, we will briefly look at the setting, mutual expectations, and sequence of events which surrounded this holy relationship.

TIME AND SPACE FOR GUIDANCE

How often did a hasid visit with his rebbe for counsel? In the early years of this charismatic Jewish movement, master and disciple engaged in frequent personal contact. While residing at the rebbe's court, the hasid would usually see his mentor for guidance at least once per month. Certain Hasidic groups, however, incorporated much less regular involvement; the Lyozhna institutions prescribed *yehidut* no more than once every three years—and only when one was unable to resolve a conflict involving two equally commendable alternatives.

Ordinarily, though, the hasic came for *yehidut* at all key junctures in his life, such as his bar mitzvah and the eve of his wedding. At such times, he sought to institute a way of divine service appropriate to his new maturity and to receive a related blessing for success. Also, throughout the hasid's life, he solicited the rebbe's assistance when confronted with a personal crisis or serious problem. Generally, aside from such urgent matters and the normal rites of passage, hasidim visited their rebbe for *yehidut* about once a year.

It should be understood that the unique character of this dialogue in part determined its frequency. For the *yehidut* was far more intense than any other helping procedure among East European Jews; there were no other encounters in which they exposed their very souls to the rebbe's scrutiny. Nor did the rebbe intend his advice to float in a social vacuum; the hasid's teacher and peers strengthened the rebbe's advice through their own encouragement and emotional support.

For such reasons, the *yehidut* was rather brief as well as infrequent by our present day standards—perhaps less than a half-hour for most people seeking guidance. Having placed tremendous faith in the rebbe's wisdom and power, the hasid had few ambivalent feelings about coming for help. As an observant Jew, he was expected to behave daily in accordance with the Law; hence, the *yehidut* tended to focus on one's specific attitude about a situation. To effect physical changes in one's economic or social world was not always possible, the rebbes emphasized. In fact, the more time a hasid required for the actual counseling session, the greater it revealed his failure to ponder thoroughly the realities of his predicament and his available options—before meeting with the rebbe.

On this intriguing subject, Rabbi Shmuel of Lubavitch offered a humorous but pointed comment. When asked why he devoted more time to the rich than the poor, he replied, "The poor know that they are poor, and their need is clear to them; so we can quickly get to the point. It takes quite a while for the rich man to see his poverty; but once we get to the point where he does, the *yehidut* takes the same amount of time."

Reflecting its deliberate and planned format, the *yehidut* typically encompassed a consistent setting. While some rebbes preferred to see the hasid during daylight hours, most adopted nightly counseling sessions. They established this arrangement not only for its convenience to those who worked during the day; rebbes also believed that nighttime is more conducive to certain kinds of communication. For the Kabbalah had long taught that time has specific subcomponents varying with the hour and season; permutations of the Divine Name revealed that from sunset until midnight, harsh decrees rule; these become sweetened by the foreshadowing of grace at dawn. The Hasidic founders felt too that one's deeper Self is more accessible at night; therefore, they preferred to deal with loftier levels of the soul during that time.

In keeping with the procession of holidays throughout the
Jewish calendar, rebbes engaged in counseling only during
certain periods of the year. While they met with their hasidim,
of course, on holiday occasions, these tended to be communal
and ritualized activities; they lacked the privacy and intimacy of the *yehidut*. Even during times of the rebbe's seasonal
quietude he could almost always be reached in true emergen-
cies through his *gabbai*.

The *yehidut* itself usually took place in the rebbe's inner
chamber. If he were traveling en route, he used a room specially prepared for him and set up according to his speci-
fications. The rebbe's chamber was ordinarily arranged so
that he sat in a thronelike chair with an unobstructed view to
the door; the distance from the desk was not great. Consistent with the meditative mood of the event, the lighting in
the room was soft, muted; candles were situated before the
rebbe. A second chair was placed near the desk so that the
visitor could sit if he wished; rarely, though, would a hasid
allow himself to do so in the rebbe's holy presence. The room
was lined with bookshelves filled with sacred volumes.

Certainly, the hasid had little time to inspect the composi-
tion of the room, the location of furniture, or other such
incidentals. His attention was wholly directed to his spiritual
master. No doubt, though, the subliminal effects of the rebbe's
chamber inspired in visitors a sense of confidence and rever-
ence conducive to the baring of one's soul. Indeed, hasidim
often referred to the *yehidut* room by such exalted aphorisms
as "the inner sanctum," "the supernal paradise," and "the
holy of holies." Even the waiting room was venerated with
such names as "the lesser paradise."

RHYTHMS OF COUNSEL

Although the *yehidut* typically represented a "crisis" rather than an ordinary event in the hasid's life, both he and the rebbe carefully prepared for the encounter. They viewed impatience and haste as antithetical to this important meeting. Indeed, the mutual preparations involved were considered an integral part of the entire event, not merely a minor prelude to it. Both participants regarded the upcoming session as serious and significant; both felt its sacred quality.

In readying himself for the *yehidut*, the rebbe would reflect in private on his mood and willingness to help those scheduled for the day. He would offer alms and fervently pray that his advice might be beneficial, directed by divine wisdom. Recognizing the great power his words would exert, the rebbe strove to free his mind from all other, potentially distracting concerns. He sought to give total, devoted attention to each person's particular problem.

Once ready to offer his guidance, the rebbe would consult with the *gabbai* concerning the people waiting outside and the order in which to admit them; often, it was the *gabbai* who actually wrote the *kvittel* (the formal request for aid and agenda for the *yehidut*), rather than the individual seeking help. Interestingly, each rebbe usually adopted a specific, preferred sequence for meeting with supplicants. Sometimes, the first to arrive at the rebbe's court were the first to see him; dignitaries enjoyed precedence over ordinary folk. The Kobriner, we are told, preferred that younger hasidim be ushered in first. And, most rebbes generally saw Gentiles before Jews—on the assumption that the contrast between the two groups would more effectively influence prayers for divine assistance to the Chosen People.

Occasionally, the rebbe might feel that a supplicant was not really prepared for the session, that he had failed to meditate sufficiently on the matter beforehand. In such instances, the rebbe would instruct the *gabbai* not to inform the hasid about this decision until the end of the day's sessions. In this manner, the individual would have gained additional hours while waiting to ponder his condition—and eventually he would be ready for the intensity of the *yehidut*.

In preparing himself for this important encounter, the hasid would visit the local *mikveh* and immerse himself in it. He typically put on his best clothes and skipped the meal prior to the *yehidut*. As he entered and sat himself in the rebbe's anteroom, he had his money ready for the *pidyon*, or ransom offering. More than simply a financial donation to sustain the rebbe's activities, the *pidyon* was imbued with mystical connotations and likened onto the holy sacrifice at the Temple of Jerusalem. Sometimes, a rebbe would refuse to use, or even accept, the *pidyon*, if he felt that it was ill-gotten gain, spiritually "tainted" by its donor's improper conduct.

Once inside the rebbe's waiting room, the hasid would write his own *kvittel* or else rely on the *gabbai* to do so. The *kvittel* was a billet on which the writer requested the rebbe's divine intercession. Among Lubavitch hasidim, the following *kvittel* formula predominated:

> To his honored Holiness, our Lord, our Teacher and our Master, may-he-live-for-many-long-days.
>
> Please do rouse the great mercies from the fount of the true mercies and graces for NAME AND MOTHER'S NAME. (Here the condition of the person for whom intercession is made is given.)
>
> Soul ransom
> *Pidyon*
>
> (Here a sum of money is mentioned.)

As the hasid waited, he would search his soul and review the major events of his life since his last *yehidut*. He dwelled on the realities of his predicament and his unfulfilled hopes; even if the session was not intended as a confessional of misdeeds, the hasid always entered the rebbe's domain as a penitent. With time permitting, the hasid would recite Psalms while waiting. Thus, before his actual encounter within the rebbe's inner chamber, the hasid was already in a heightened state of consciousness—filled with images of his life and the rebbe's strength and wisdom.

Suddenly, the *gabbai* would call the hasid's name. His heart would beat faster as he tensed up. With his free hand, he might smooth his beard and adjust his clothes. Touching with a fervent kiss the *mezuzoh* at the doorpost, he would step into the rebbe's chamber, and approaching his desk, hand him the *kvittel* and *pidyon*. The *yehidut* had begun.

MOMENTS OF SPLENDOR

Let us imagine ourselves with the hasid and rebbe. Close your eyes for a moment and in your visualization you too are now in the rebbe's chamber.

With a kindly and thoughtful look, the rebbe takes the items from the hasid's outstretched hand. Placing the *pidyon* into an open drawer, the rebbe slowly surveys the hasid, who stands nearby, refusing to sit down even when invited to do so. The hasid's clothes, stance, appearance, and facial expression—all of these the rebbe examines with care.

As he turns to the *kvittel*, he gazes at the name and uses a mnemonic device to remember it. Having stilled his mind prior to the meeting, the rebbe now feels a surge of impressions flowing through him, taking him to the root of the hasid's soul. Before reading further, the rebbe begins to sense the real needs of the hasid—not those necessarily listed on the *kvittel*—as well as how those needs can best be fulfilled.

The rebbe perceives the soul in front of him as it stood in the fullness of the original, divine plan—and the blocks and hindrances that are keeping the soul from advancement.

Looking deeply into the *kvittel*, the rebbe examines its manifest content and compares it with his estimate of what could have been written. He also notices whether the *gabbai* or the hasid wrote it. Shifting the focus of his eyes, the rebbe gazes at the entire *kvittel*, turns away, then looks again.

The Hebrew letters seem to dance and sway, forming new patterns of hidden meaning. The rebbe begins to sense further revelations about the other's soul; he feels the presence of the departed ancestors who have spiritually accompanied the hasid to this sacred encounter. For a timeless instant, the rebbe integrates all of this within; he becomes the hasid, and standing in his place, sees how far the hasid is from being able to accept the right counsel for himself. Flooded with immense compassion, the rebbe sighs. Simultaneously, he meditates on his own life and seeks a corresponding experience to the hasid's predicament.

Blushing with embarrassment at the rebbe's sigh, the hasid is sorry for the grief and concern for his soul he has caused. He is about to apologize, but the rebbe has begun his questioning. He inquires about the hasid's family and background, livelihood, and progress in study and prayer. Some questions seem remote from the matter of the *kvittel*, but the hasid diligently offers his replies.

The rebbe takes one of the hasid's answers and repeats it to him, either in the same manner, or with a different inflection. Thus, the rebbe begins to elevate the communication to a higher plane, from which he can give the *ezah* or prescription for action. As the hasid appears ready, having already experienced the shock of insight through the rebbe's repetitive remarks, the next stage of the session is reached. First, though, the rebbe quotes a few relevant words from the Torah.

The hasid thereupon sees that the rebbe is about to offer his counsel, as he has shifted in his seat. His face takes on more authoritative lines as his voice becomes commanding and yet remains compassionate. The hasid is "all ears" to absorb the *ezah*.

Having finished his counsel lasting several minutes, the rebbe permits the hasid to ask questions clarifying his mentor's comments. Some of these seem strangely unrelated to the hasid's problem, but he trusts in the rebbe's guidance. In an act of faith, he now stands near and inclines his head for the blessing. Again, the rebbe alters his expression and manner; alert to this shift, the hasid strains to catch every syllable of the blessing.

When the rebbe has concluded his blessing, the hasid utters a fervent "Amen," and starts to move backward. Without turning his back to his master, and without averting his gaze, the hasid backs toward the door. The *yehidut* is over.

The rebbe makes a few notations on the *kvittel*, placing it where he can later use it to intercede for the hasid. Stepping out of the rebbe's chamber, the hasid is suddenly accosted by others. As they eagerly question him with, "Nu? What did the rebbe tell you?" he fixes the details in his mind, still aroused from the power of the rebbe's assistance.

THE ART OF DIAGNOSIS

In the forementioned, diagnostic phase of the *yehidut*, the rebbe had to deal with many coordinates in locating the hasid at his particular focus of existence. The rebbe sought to pinpoint the hasid's precise spiritual rung and plot his movement along that level. In accomplishing this, the rebbe made use of a spectrum of informative indicators—ranging from the hasid's ethnic origin and socioeconomic status, to his bodily type and intellectual bent, to his degree of inner discipline and religious commitment. The rebbe had to integrate all of

these factors before deciding on how to respond to the plea
for his aid.

Certainly, the *kvittel* itself provided several diagnostic clues
which the rebbe typically read with anticipation. Would the
kvittel be a complaining one? Its very length may already have
signalled this, for the longer it was, the more wary the rebbe
became. He felt that if the hasid were bringing too many
circumstantial details to the *yehidut*, the less he truly understood his situation and the greater the likelihood that he
would be defensive when questioned. In contrast, the rebbe
interpreted a brief *kvittel* as revealing a higher degree of trust
in the *yehidut* (and in God) and a simpler approach to the
vicissitudes of life. The presence of numerous antecedents
and causes on the *kvittel* indicated that the hasid expected to
be advised only on his own terms.

Nevertheless, the rebbe preferred even a lengthy *kvittel* to a
verbal diatribe; matters could be resolved far more easily if
the hasid did not need to first "work his story out" in the
rebbe's presence. Taking this risk, though, the hasid's mentor
sometimes asked him to state exactly what he wanted—despite
what he had already written on the *kvittel*. The rebbe did this
to allow the hasid to *feel* what he had recorded and not
merely parrot empty sentiments—for in such cases, one gained
little from the sacred dialogue.

Not surprisingly, rebbes delighted in *kvittels* that were spiritual in focus (known as *Baal Shemesque kvittel*)—but only if
these were genuine and not merely gestures for approval. For
instance, to a person who presented an obviously insincere
request for spiritual enlightenment, Rabbi Menachem Mendel I of Lubavitch retorted, "Fool! Only this you lack?" At
one point in time, Rabbi Schneur Zalman refused all but
"spiritual" *kvittels*; he insisted that his function was not to
procure material blessings for supplicants—that God appor-
tions to each person the appropriate amount of wealth. Rabbi
Mendel of Kotzk likewise refused to intercede when his followers sought help for such mundane problems as the health
of their livestock.

Generally, though, the Hasidic rebbe recognized that few

kvittels directed to him would encompass lofty subjects; he acutely understood the hardships suffered by *shtetl* folk. If the *kvittel* was concerned with ill health, the rebbe was quick to commiserate and offer his intercession. If the *kvittel* related to childlessness, the rebbe would likewise commiserate, though before he "promised" children, he was rather circumspect. But if the *kvittel* focused on livelihood and finances, the rebbe was much slower to offer empathy and promises for intercession; he might feel that "Israel's poverty becomes him"—that the hasid ultimately benefited from his economic difficulties.

Signs without Speech

Having read the manifest part of the *kvittel*, the rebbe would set it aside, to return to it later. He would next turn his full attention from the small billet to the hasid's living presence. Within a brief span, rarely longer than a minute or two, the rebbe would absorb voluminous sensory and extrasensory information emanating from the figure standing before him. From such stimuli, the rebbe would move decisively to the question-and-answer phase of the encounter.

The *Targum* translates the Biblical phrase, "a living soul," into "a spirit that speaks." But it is not only the spirit that speaks; the body does too. In *shtetl* times as in our own, the language of the human body was often more eloquent than that of the mind. Consequently, the rebbe would concentrate keenly on the hasid's nonverbal, physical cues—especially his posture and stance.

As part of the *yehidut*'s protocol, the hasid was expected to stand in a posture of awe and submission to his rebbe. Yet, the rebbe was highly sensitive to whether this posture appeared customary or forced by the occasion. He knew that the proud man stands more self-consciously when assuming the posture of a supplicant; the same stance fits the beggar like

an old shoe. Our habitual bearing is observable when when
we assume another stance; certainly, the ordinary *shtetl* Jew
was no trained actor, able to camouflage his characteristic
body language. Thus, the rebbe scrutinized this nonverbal
realm like an open book.

Similarly, the rebbe learned much about the hasid by the
clothes he wore. Each Hasidic group typically adopted its
own distinctive garb; the group to which one belonged was
readily identifiable by one's clothes. Indeed, if a hasid changed
any aspects of the "uniform," he demonstrated his criticism
or dissent from the group.

In coming to the rebbe, the hasid was expected to wear his
best clothes; otherwise, he opened himself to criticism from
peers. Consequently, the rebbe was able to observe the hasid's
conformity or noncomformity to the group's norms. If the
hasid appeared self-conscious in his garb, the rebbe knew that
it was unnatural to the hasid, not his normal attire. The rebbe
examined too the amount of wear-and-tear on the hasid's
clothes—as a sign of his financial state, as well as an indicator
of his character traits. In short, the rebbe gleaned a great deal
of information about the hasid from the seemingly insignificant factors of his body language and apparel.

But the rebbe also looked to extrasensory cues to diagnose
and counsel most effectively. According to early Hasidism,
what inhabits the body is not the whole soul, which is too
vast to be contained within physical bounds. Yet, the soul is
affected by the happenings of the body and reveals these
through a paranormal aura, we are told. On this subject, the
Maggid of Mezritch once stated, "A tiny hole in the body
bespeaks a large one in the soul."

Therefore, the rebbe carefully inspected the transphysical
aura that surrounded the hasid. Through the rebbe's questioning gaze, he discerned bodily diseases and emotional traumas.
Sometimes, based on what he saw, he recommended that the
hasid immediately visit a physician. And if the doctor were
unable to find any trace of the disease, the rebbe might
suggest to him where to follow up with a more intensive
examination.

Socioeconomic Factors

Once the rebbe began his questioning of the hasid, many more indicators loomed into perspective. In fact, from the first words the hasid uttered, he transmitted valuable clues about his background and personality. For the rebbe was immensely aided by his ability to discern the hasid's ethnic origin—and thereby guage, at least partially, the amount of warmth in the hasid's upbringing. Among East European Jewry as a whole, there were wide variations in cultural outlook depending on one's region of origin; people from different ethnic groups observed particular norms for familial expressiveness and affection.

Consequently, the rebbe counseled with images and phrases consistent with the hasid's specific ethnic temperament. If the hasid spoke in one dialect, but affected the garb of another ethnic group, this fact too served as a key to his personality. Generally, the rebbe relied on the individual's ethnic origin to reinforce his loyalty to Hasidism. If the two figures shared the same cultural background, their intimacy was especially warm.

For instance, Zalman Schachter several years ago had an interview with the contemporary Bobover Rebbe, Rabbi Shlomo Halberstamm. The Bobover Rebbe related a parable, after which he assumed an intimate manner of speech. "Your father is a Galitzianer, is he not?" the Rebbe asked. Upon receiving an affirmative reply, he mused, "Toss a stick into the air, and it falls on its root."

Along these lines, the early Hasidic rebbe sought to locate each supplicant environmentally. For what was normal behavior in a large city was abnormal in a small village. By understanding the hasid's ordinary habitat, the rebbe was able to judge whether the particular way-of-life was appropriate or not. Just as Rabbi Schmuel of Lubavitch found in his hasid's environmental situation an opportunity to lead him to insight, so too did other rebbes utilize rural models for rural hasidim and urban models for city dwellers.

On this intriguing subject, a more contemporary Lubavitch rebbe observed that, "The place of one's domicile . . . exerts a fundamental influence on one's style of life. It influences all branches of life from the . . . development of one's talents and the manifestation of one's soul powers, to the interpersonal area. . . . If the influence of the environment itself is so great, even greater is the influence of [its] social mores." Thus, the rebbe hardly counseled in the identical manner a remote villager and a Warsaw merchant, traveling, say, to Danzig and Leipzig regularly for business. To do so would have missed the mark.

Yet another major diagnostic realm for the rebbe was the hasid's involvement with family and friends, his social network. The *shtetl* world fostered a great deal of warmth among Jews, but it also produced problems of conflicting loyalties; some folk found it difficult to meet all the demands on their time. In response to this situation, certain rebbes, like Nachman of Bratslav, insisted on the validity of each person's daily need for privacy and self-reflection. "Consider what you are doing," he advised, "and ponder whether it is worthy that you devote your life to it." Yet, even such staunch advocates for solitude recognized that the yearning for the contemplative life sometimes hid the wish to escape from necessary obligations to family and others.

Thus, if the hasid planned to remain at the rebbe's quarters for any length of time, the rebbe first ascertained whether the hasid had his wife's consent. And, in deciding the hasid's suitable penitential donation, the rebbe would carefully determine the hasid's financial situation—so as to impose only a bearable burden on him and his family.

The *kvittel* itself provided helpful clues to the hasid's social situation—listing by name his parents and children and what each one lacked, so that all might receive the rebbe's blessing. Consequently, the *kvittel* served as a sociogram, mirroring the hasid's loyalties and conflicts; it indicated these either by the overt request for aid or the order in which the names were written. For example, the hasid's seemingly simple expression of hope that his unwed daughter would find a "good match" accorded the rebbe material for further questions. He knew that the hasid was concerned not only about the marriage, but also about the finances necessary to provide his daughter's dowry. In such instances, the rebbe translated the hasid's social need into a monetary one as well, and dealt with each in relation to the other.

The rebbe also examined the sorts of problems the hasid related about his friends' predicaments. When called upon to offer his blessing or advice for a friend, the rebbe probed the hasid's personal view on the matter. Did he judge his friend too harshly or too leniently? Was he compassionate or intolerant? Such information revealed much about the hasid's own outlook on life, and suggested ways to provide him with insight. On this point, an interesting story is told.

To a hasid who complained about his friend, calling him a hypocrite, Rabbi Menachem Mendel I of Lubavitch replied, "How long have you known him?" When the hasid answered that he had known the man twenty-five years, Rabbi Menachem Mendel asked, "And all that time he has acted the same way?" The hasid nodded. Thereupon, Rabbi Menachem Mendel took a sharp blade and cut into the table, showing the hasid how it was stained through and through.

"This table has been painted now for twenty years," Rabbi Menachem Mendel commented. "Every year before Passover it is sanded and stained. The stain has now completely penetrated the wood. Isn't it possible that this hypocrite or "stained one" is now authentically as he claims to be?"

Certainly, in their impoverished and oppressed existence, the Jews of Eastern Europe were often confronted with severe economic hardships. Thus, as part of the rebbe's diagnostic procedure, he typically looked at how the hasid managed his worldly commitments. The mature individual discharged his financial obligations as efficiently as possible; earning his livelihood with sincere effort and exertion, he nevertheless remembered all the while where his true "home" lay.

The rebbe considered as "kosher" material involvement as
a means, but not as an end in itself. If the hasid began to
become preoccupied with such matters, he was in danger of
forgetting his primary allegiance, to the service of the Almighty.

Another tale speaks precisely to this issue. A hasid once
complained to Rabbi Shmuel of Lubavitch that he found himself no longer able to study well; his prayers had become
mechanical and lifeless. The rebbe asked the hasid where he
resided (though he knew very well the circumstances of the
Hasid's domicile). The hasid replied that he lived in Byeshenkowich. When the rebbe asked where the hasid did his
business, he replied, "In Riga."

"And how many months do you spend in Riga?" the rebbe
asked.

"Ten and one-half months," the hasid answered.

"If you spend ten and one-half months in Riga and only one
and one-half months in Byeshenkowich," the rebbe queried,
"why then do you say that you live in Byeshenkowich?"

"Rebbe," the hasid replied, "In Riga, I am for business; but
in Byeshenkowich, I am at home."

And suddenly, the hasid understood the rebbe's meaning.
The hasid had forsaken his domicile in Torah study and
prayer and had taken up residence in business.

It should be understood that the rebbe was not concerned
so much with the hasid's livelihood and income as their
concomitant and related problems. In the *shtetl* milieu, there
was little social mobility. For the most part, men assumed the
vocations of their fathers. To do so was the safest choice,
since there would be *hazaqah*, a strong claim, impervious to
legal challenge, to one's taking on one's father's trade. For a
variety of reasons, though, a man might refuse to adopt his
father's vocation—even though well suited to it. Perhaps, the
son was rebelling against parental authority in a self-destructive
way. Thus, the rebbe had to be sensitive to the hasid's attitude about his work.

Generally, a wealthy hasid was not expected to adopt the
same lifestyle as a pauper; the rebbe felt that what is luxury
and a sign of irresponsibility among those with limited

resources, is the customary ménage of the rich. Nevertheless, while the rebbe expected a degree of arrogance from the wealthy, their attitude was to reflect their actual financial situation. For example, we are told that a rich man once publicly defied a rabbinical assembly. Thereupon, a rabbi pointedly rebuked him by declaring, "Solomon said, 'The rich answered with arrogance.' But your arrogance, it would seem, greatly exceeds your wealth."

The hasid's capacity to handle his material status thus revealed a great deal about his character. If he was so inept at managing his worldly obligations that he was heavily dependent—in other words, a *shlemiel*—the rebbe could respond to him in either of two ways. If the rebbe knew that the man could not be trusted with higher levels of responsibility, he could be nursed along at his present pace. But if the rebbe suspected that the man's dependence was merely a lazy avoidance of duty, he was left alone to learn from sinking or swimming through his own efforts.

The Hasidic leaders stressed that when one uses his financial position to benefit others—and thus, ultimately, serve the Holy One—he accrues great merit for himself and for all Jews. For example, a young woman once received a long overdue payment, amounting to more than her family's savings and, by that time, she had a large family to care for. She obtained her husband's consent to turn over the entire sum to the rebbe. He used the money to establish a special loan fund for *yeshiva* teachers. The woman's generous act represented heroic virtue in the eyes of the whole Hasidic community and served as an outstanding moral example, though the rebbe never divulged her name. Such virtue shone as more than a personality indicator to the rebbe; it provided a source of merit by which he strove to arouse divine grace and mercy.

SPIRITUAL SIGNPOSTS

The rebbe relied on a host of indicators to effectively diagnose the hasid's predicament. Yet, without doubt, his spiritual state was the most important sign to the rebbe, who characteristically regarded the inner world as the crucial one. A hasid might be poor, he might suffer from ill health; perhaps, his family complained that he spent too little time with them. But the rebbe viewed such concerns as only secondary to the hasid's ultimate purpose on earth: to serve the Almighty in uplifting the holy sparks of existence. For this reason, he carefully examined the hasid's spiritual attainment—as shown by his Torah knowledge, his quality of prayer, and his *kavanah*, or sacred intentionality.

Torah Knowledge

While the Baal Shem Tov and his disciples proclaimed to *shtetl* folk that scholarship is not the only path to the divine, these founders never denigrated Torah study. Otherwise, such brilliant Talmudic thinkers as the Maggid of Mezritch would scarcely have been won over to the Hasidic cause. He realized that the Besht's stress on serving God with joy and delight was hardly antithetical to fervent learning. Each person should use his talents to bring the celestial splendor closer to earth; for one with an active mind, this means scholarship.

In fact, many Hasidic leaders, like Rabbi Schneur Zalman, explicitly extolled intellectual prowess as a way to the Holy

Source. He emphasized that one of the pillars on which the world stands is Torah; the very purpose of creation—God's "hiding" in order to be found—is realized through Torah mastery. By penetrating its secrets, he stressed, great supernal mysteries are revealed. Similarly, Rabbi Nachman of Bratslav advised his followers, "You should travel everywhere in the Torah. In the Future Life, you will then be able to boast that you have visited every place in our sacred literature.... At that time, you will also be able to remember everything that you have ever learned."

Consequently, the rebbe sought to discern the hasid's depth of Torah understanding. At what level did he approach its varying topography? Was his knowledge superficial or did it show true, creative thought? Interestingly, the Hasidic founders taught that because many souls had in past lives already learned much of the Torah's normative features, they needed to confront its esoteric, loftier side. The rebbe insisted that one capable of advanced study but who dealt only with lower planes of the Torah was not fulfilling his true inner potential.

The really crucial issues in a hasid's Torah involvement, though, were his degree of exertion and effort. These personality traits were prized far more than his sheer power of intellect. In a sense, this view is what at least partly divided the hasidim from the *Mitnaggedim*, their opponents, who accepted abstruse scholarship without fervor. Therefore, the hasid who tended to over-intellectualize the Torah might be shocked to find during the *yehidut* that he was not as inwardly proficient as he had believed.

For example, a Chabad hasid once came to visit Rabbi Mendel of Kotzk. In the course of their discussion, the rebbe asked the man what the prayers really meant to him. The hasid launched into an elaborate discourse derived from intense study. Impatiently, Rabbi Mendel interrupted, "That's all very well. That is what it means to your head. But what does it mean to your *puppik* (belly-button)?"

Many rebbes actively promulgated this attitude—that spirituality involves one's whole being and not merely the intellect. A mature hasid did not permit a great distance to exist be-

tween his mental acuity and his daily conduct; he knew that
the realms of Torah and *mitzvot* had to be in harmony. In a
like manner, the rebbe looked closely at the hasid's degree of
observance and commitment to the Jewish Law. The traditional dictum, "He fulfilled his obligation," was not enough
for the hasid, who was expected to do more than the Law
required; elsewise, he was guilty of mere automatism.

Prayer: The Divine Channel

Within the hasid's spiritual space, his devotion to prayer
was regarded with great significance. While the Baal Shem
Tov and his adherents venerated Torah study, they esteemed
fervent prayer to the Holy One as an end in itself—so much
so that Rabbi Pinhas of Koretz declared, "Prayer is not to
God; prayer *is* God." Indeed, the key distinguishing feature
of early Hasidism may have been its tremendous emphasis on
prayer as an ecstatic experience, capable of transporting each
person to divine realms of splendor.

In his diagnosis, therefore, the rebbe carefully examined
the depth and intensity of the hasid's prayer life. Was he
simply mouthing pious words? Or, could he surrender his ego
and feel the hidden worlds draw near? Was he able to plunge
fearlessly into this region of paradox without clinging to false
stability? For the Hasidic sages truly advocated an approach
to prayer transcending duality.

The hasid was expected to divest himself fully from worldly
attachments, yet be able to heed the cry of a child. He was to
seek the loftiest, celestial, and angelic aspects of the Hebrew
letters before him, yet "pray with his prayer desk in mind."
He was urged to find something "new" in each prayer, yet
resist the temptation to search for mere clever homilies. He
was admonished to view human history as ultimately only a
subspecies of the divine procession, yet feel the deep distress
of the people for whom he interceded.

The rebbe looked at whether the hasid experienced prayer not only as a time of surrender, but also as "a time of warfare." Like the Biblical Jacob, who wrestled in crisis with the angel, the hasid was expected to struggle and prevail against his own lesser impulses. Whenever "extraneous" thoughts—such as those related to sexual or material matters—flitted through his consciousness, he was encouraged to repel these as dangerous invaders. In so doing, he could return to soaring in the highest spheres within his attainment.

The rebbe was also concerned with the fruits of the hasid's activity. After praying, did he show increased compassion for others? Did he glean from his heavenly communion any living words to be realized in the tasks of that day? And, was he thereupon imbued with greater strength and will to perform the *mitzvot*, the sacred commandments?

The hasid who could manage all this had achieved a high degree of receptivity. Prayer had become the laboratory whereby he prepared himself for the rebbe's counsel. Each hasid was thus scrutinized for his ability to pray without artifice or pretense, in accordance with the Baal Shem Tov's inspiring practice. Because the *yehidut* was set in the very context of the liturgical day at the rebbe's court, no hasid could escape this dramatic confrontation with Hasidic prayer.

Kavanah: The Power of Intentionality

In an integrally related manner, the rebbe's spiritual diagnosis focused on the hasid's overall *kavanah*, or intentionality. Encompassing far more than mere willpower, this term was an exalted one in classic Hasidic teaching; its literal meaning was "to direct" or "to aim," for it was the rebbe's task to help his hasid channel his energies outward and upward in divine service. *Kavanah* reflected the person's capacity to achieve a sustained, "one-pointedness" of concentration on the transcendent aspects of existence. As Rabbi Schneur Zalman tersely

Believing that her plea had been rejected, the mother left and broke down in great lament. One of the Kotzker's chief disciples, seeing her plight, sought to console her. He explained that Rabbi Mendel had used the argument that her son "had scarcely begun" his tasks as a means to appeal to the celestial powers to prolong the boy's life. With this understanding, the mother was consoled.

The rebbe also looked at the hasid's tendency toward growth or stagnation as a theme related to his past lives. If the hasid appeared static in exercising his talents, the rebbe might point to these skills as attainments from another lifetime. He would also interpret the hasid's refusal to advance as a desire to rest on earlier laurels. Diagnostically, though, this discernment was not an easy one for the rebbe to make. He had to decide whether the soul before him was indeed idle in its development, or else groping toward new goals and challenges.

One clue was the hasid's outlook on his life. The rebbe translated emotional rigidity and stubbornness as signs of blockage, or even a stranglehold, exerted by one's past existence. If the hasid were truly attracted to a new path, his perspective would be more fluid, his striving would have less structure. In responding, the rebbe would seek to give form to the hasid's emerging yearnings for change and direction. Sometimes, there were genuine borderland cases in which a soul had to work through a pattern of activity harmonious with, but not identical to, that of a past life. While the rebbe regarded such a case as difficult both diagnostically and therapeutically, he relied on his powers of assessment to insure the correct way of guidance.

Early in the rebbe's calling, he typically spent more time in the *yehidut* than he did as he grew more experienced. Initially, he had to integrate rather consciously and deliberately all of the forementioned sensory and extrasensory indicators. However, he gradually learned to shift more responsibility to his *ruah hakodesh*, the holy inner Source. Also, as he became more diagnostically proficient, he developed greater empathy; he could better sense each soul's uniqueness, its particular needs and earthly purpose.

In this manner, the rebbe synthesized all aspects of the hasid standing near him. The past, present, and future reverberated like sparks in the rebbe's mind as he mused over his course of action, for he had to find the right door that still barred the hasid. In their timeless encounter, the rebbe was at last ready to grasp the key and open the inner gates.

CHAPTER FIVE

INNER
TRANSFORMATIONS

*To Rabbi Menachem Mendel I of Lubavitch, a hasid once came to
complain, "Everyone in the House of Study steps on me." Rabbi
Menachem Mendel said to him, "Who asked you to spread yourself
all over the House of Study, so that everywhere one steps, one has to
step on you?"*

—Hasidic oral tradition

*Thought is in man's hands. He can bend it as he wills, to wherever
he wills. . . . One's thoughts may wander, flying and plunging through
many strange and extraneous ideas. But if man concentrates on
proper things, he has the power to bend thought and lead it back to
the straight way.*

—Rabbi Nachman of Bratlsav

HAVING COMPLETED THE DIAGNOSTIC PHASE of the *yehidut*,
the Hasidic rebbe was ready to offer his specific prescription
for action. He felt sure that he had penetrated to the root of
the hasid's dilemma; with divine favor, only the necessary
deeds needed to be enacted for a successful solution to the
problem at hand. Yet, before the rebbe could extend his counsel,

114

he first had to arouse the hasid into a receptive mood, an openness to the need for immediate personal growth. For without such conscious intent, the hasid would make little real progress.

How did the rebbe accomplish this challenging task? In *shtetl* times as in our own, few people wished to break comfortable habits or undertake far-reaching changes in their lives. The prospect of having to deliberately negate long-standing patterns of behavior and instill new ones rarely is a pleasant one. Indeed, most persons came to the rebbe for approval and confirmation of their way-of-life, not for painful self-examination. If the rebbe merely complied with the hasid's requests and gratified these, much of the effectiveness of the *yehidut* was lost.

After all, the rebbe saw himself not as one who sold his hasid only "grease for his wheels." The rebbe's real merchandise was Torah, *mitzvot*, and assistance to do *teshuvah*. Advice in mundane matters and blessings for health, children, and wealth were bonuses and premiums added to the real business of growth and guidance.

Thus, the rebbe utilized a variety of methods to heighten the hasid's desire for inner change. Not only within the counseling session itself, but also outside of it, the rebbe emphasized the capacity of each person to initiate dramatic changes in one's life. In his many public discourses, the rebbe frequently expounded on this important theme and extolled the power of human intentionality and will. The writings of major Hasidic thinkers like the Maggid of Mezritch, Rabbi Schneur Zalman of Liady, and many others repeatedly stressed that lower human impulses can be overcome decisively and bent to serve the higher, if the individual wills it.

ACTIVATING CHANGE

The Besht and his adherents taught that each person has the potential to alter at any time old ways of thinking and behaving. Habits can be powerful, they recognized, but are always subservient to one's conscious mind. "Every individual has free will to do as he desires," declared Rabbi Nachman of Bratslav. "Free will is the ability to do something if you want to, and the ability to refrain from something . . .[if that is what you need to do]." The Baal Shem Tov and others often told stories that vividly illustrated this point. In such tales, even those long ensnared by their destructive impulses succeed in reaching new realms of harmony through their sincere effort and faith in the Almighty.

Some rebbes prescribed specific meditative techniques to strengthen the intentionality of their hasidim. For example, Rabbi Elimelekh of Lizensk recommended that each day after the *yehidut* one should visualize himself in the rebbe's presence, as he awesomely intones his holy words of guidance. In this way, the hasid would find his willpower increased, Rabbi Elimelekh taught.

The day-to-day conduct of the Hasidic rebbe provided further motivation for the hasid to remain open to personal change. In many respects, the rebbe served as a living example of spontaneity, so that his hasidim would often exclaim in wonderment, "His footsteps are unknown. . . . Who can understand his ways?" Like the writer Peretz's Litwak, the rebbe was seen to ascend daily to heaven, "if not higher." To the citified Warsovian hasid, addicted to urban conformity, Rabbi Ahrele Hopstein of Kozhinitz was an unfathomable enigma. Through his startling antics, he made self-change the norm for his hasidim.

Because of the rebbe's exalted position within the Hasidic milieu, he was able to catalyze effectively the growth of his followers. No matter how radical his prescription for action, the rebbe's word, no matter how unusual, carried with the power of an unshakable decree. To be accepted by the community, a hasid had only to announce that he was behaving in accordance with his master's instructions. In our own society, of course, no therapist's suggestions possess as much authority. Knowing that his observance of the rebbe's advice would be respected by all, the hasid had much less reason to fear personal innovation in his life. Consequently, even a great scholar of Torah could agree for spiritual motives to serve as a coachman, without losing any face over his altered social position.

In short, the hasid who changed his role at the rebbe's behest did not "die" socially. Only in rare cases did the rebbe impose exile on the hasid. When this unusual event occurred, it indeed meant social death for a certain period. Nevertheless, the hasid's "resurrection" was assured, together with his ultimate uplifting of status in the entire community.

The hasid's receptivity to change was reinforced not only through his veneration of the rebbe, but also through his involvement with a *haver* or special friend. This relationship was an extremely important one in the Hasidic world, for the *haver* helped to plan the *yehidut* and then was informed of the rebbe's counsel. By sharing with his friend the rebbe's comments and advice, the hasid gained a strong ally in his struggle for a new direction. In turn, by serving as a daily reminder of the rebbe's guidance, the friend became the master's surrogate.

Despite such aids to the hasid's advancement to wholeness, the rebbe often preferred for one to change slowly for lasting success. To initiate this gradual process, the rebbe sometimes set up a series of little nudges, enabling the hasid to accommodate the larger change into his life. Generally, though, the rebbe was not overly concerned about the likelihood that his counsel would be spurned. His moral authority and the hasid's wish to comply, the blessing and the results that the hasid desired—all favored the forces of growth. And, the rebbe knew that his own reputation was not at stake: the hasid who would not comply with the *yehidut*'s prescription was aware that his failure would be attributed to him alone, not his master.

Interestingly, the rebbe also bore in mind his hasid's tendency to overdo the advice, thereby rendering it absurd. For instance, having been asked to speak kind words to everyone he met, the hasid might become ridiculously over-solicitious, even offensively so. Such behavior, the rebbe knew, might indicate a hidden wish to undermine his advice. Thus, in order to avoid this trap, the rebbe might put a limiting "rider" onto his counsel. Indeed, the skillful rebbe had many tools to effect the change he saw as necessary.

In the sections to follow, we will concentrate on some of the intriguing ways in which the rebbe managed the emotional ebb and flow within the *yehidut*. Such methods, all predicated upon unconditional love, included catharsis, confession, shock, restructuring, arrangement-making, and dream analysis. We should emphasize, though, that without exception, the rebbe expected his hasid to grow in accordance with the dictates of Jewish Law and Hasidic practice; for both rebbe and hasid, no other form of personal change was permissible.

LOVE: ENERGY FOR WHOLENESS

Without doubt, love was the key ingredient in the relationship between the rebbe and his hasid. It was a vibrant, surging force transcending mere acceptance or respect; in fact, Hasidim knew that *ahavat Yisroel* ("love of Israel") was a divine commandment from the Torah. This great love energized their moments together and allowed the depth and scope of the *yehidut* to exist.

If the hasid felt the absence of this sacred quality, he would not have been able to bare his very soul. Nor would the rebbe have attained such empathic identification with the other's problems. Hasidic leaders therefore expounded on the importance of this celestial energy. The Maggid of Mezritch declared that he wished he could love his own children as much as the Besht had loved even the most wicked in Israel—and the love of the Maggid for his son, "the Angel," was proverbial.

Rabbi Moshe Leib of Sassove taught that one who could not with equanimity suck the puss from another's wound, had not yet come to understand this love. He explained that he had personally learned from two peasants at an inn that "to love means to know what the other lacks." Similarly, Rabbi Abraham Joshua Heschel of Apt said that he wished to be known as the *Oheb Yisroel* ("the lover of Israel"). He considered this appellation the supreme epitaph.

Yet, inevitably, in accepting the hasid's whole being, the rebbe had to deal with subtle, psychological complexities—especially internalized figures from the hasid's past. In an illustrative anecdote, a young hasid came to the rebbe for help with a predicament. The rebbe intuitively sensed that the problem belonged not to the young man, but to his teacher. Thereupon, the rebbe sent for the *mashpiyah*, who was rebuked for transferring his difficulties onto the young hasid.

The rebbe treated parental vestiges in the hasid far more deliberately. In part, the rebbe did not wish to remove such introjections completely since they often provided great benefit to the hasid. One could not easily say, "My God, and God of my fathers," if he lacked warm, parental images. Thus, the rebbe separated the hasid from his parental introjections only if these interfered with his inner growth.

For instance, the rebbe might report that he had spoken with the discarnate soul of the hasid's father or other ancestor—and had obtained agreement to the counsel. Hasidim did not question the rebbe's power to do so; in fact, stories abound that celebrate such divine strength. We are told that in a disciple's dream, the soul of the "Ari," Rabbi Isaac Luria, appeared to the Besht and they argued over an interpretation

of Torah; the "Ari" finally acceded to the Besht's viewpoint.
Later, the Besht asked his disciple to corroborate his interpretation by telling his dream.

In counseling, the rebbe not only dealt with parental
introjections, but with other figures, too. It was relatively
rare for a hasid to switch to another rebbe; but if the hasid
did so, he usually had internalized many attitudes and styles
of behavior through his earlier, unsuccessful relationship. In
such cases, the new rebbe had to handle these old patterns
before he could spark a meaningful encounter. By personify-
ing the hasid's past misdeeds in the form of evil entities, the
rebbe also helped him. That way, the hasid could face the
dark or seemingly demonic side of his own personality.

In keeping with Kabbalistic practice, the rebbe also addressed the hasid's being in the transcendent world. Earlier
in this book we have looked at this provocative dimension of
classic Hasidism. Suffice it to say here that the rebbe strove
to open the necessary gates and channels to aid the hasid. For
example, if the person needed to be healed, the rebbe sought
to awaken the appropriate forces from the realm of health.
Sometimes, the rebbe might find the direct celestial path
blocked. In such instances, he strove to unlock an indirect
channel by devious means.

A hasid suffering from a fatal disease found no help until
he came to Rabbi Pinhas of Koretz, who wished him great
wealth. The rebbe later explained that when he found the
gates of well-being blocked, he thereupon opened the gates of
abundance. Once he had achieved this, he was able to secure
for the hasid a new lease on life.

Reflecting his all-encompassing love, the rebbe saw the
hasid as one growing and evolving—not as a stationary entity.
In this sense, the rebbe glimpsed the potentials that lay dormant and envisioned their eventual splendor within the other's
existence. In essence, the rebbe viewed the hasid's personal
situation as part of the great, cosmic process of *tiqun*, or
upraising of all the fallen sparks: everything yearned to unite
with the divine Source. As Rabbi Schneur Zalman of Liady
observed, "Therefore is man named 'one who walks,' and not,

'one who stands in one place.' He must rise from rung to rung and not remain fixed at one station."

Hasidic leaders emphasized that this internal ascent is not always a smooth one. Rebbes knew that "between one level and the next, before one can reach the higher one, he must 'fall' from the previous rung." In these moments, the hasid indeed felt stricken with despair and hopelessness; he feared that his difficulty might endure forever—and desperately sought the rebbe's solace.

The hasid's mentor then had to use all his empathy, to ask himself how it felt to be seemingly forever arrested at this stage and fear that the situation would never change. He had to be able to fully experience the hasid's anguish, yet remain aware that the problem was, after all, only transitory. For the rebbe knew that "man is judged anew each day" and that tomorrow would be a different time.

A beautiful Hasidic tale expresses this perspective. We are told that once the Besht's disciples asked him to resolve the apparent contradiction between the sayings of the sages that, "Man's budget is granted to him from Rosh Hashonah to Rosh Hashonah" and "Man is judged anew each day." The Besht responded by knocking on his window and calling to the water-carrier.

"Yuckel, tell me how are you today?" asked the Besht.

"Oy, rebbe!" Yuckel sighed. "I am old and my shoulders are weak. The children are busy studying Torah and not one thinks to help me. My wife is old and sick. My sons-in-law conduct themselves like rabbis, but all falls on my shoulders, rebbe. I don't want to sin, but I feel depressed by all my woe."

The next day, the Besht called him again, as the hasidim watched. "And, how do you feel today?" the Besht asked.

Yuckel chuckled and said, "Rebbe, you know, I am a lucky man. I have fine children and sons-in-law who study Torah. My wife, she is such a darling and keeps house well, even though she is old and sick. And to think of it—all this is borne on these old shoulders! Yes, rebbe, I am a lucky man. May God be praised for His abundant graces."

After Yuckel left, the Besht turned to his disciples. "You see," he said, "not a single thing has changed. Yuckel is the same and his budget unvarying, but today he was judged differently."

THE REBBE'S PAIN

Despite the rebbe's skill as an advisor, he could not completely avoid experiencing some of the hasid's pain. Indeed, the Hasidic founders taught that to be effective, the rebbe had to identify with the hasid's problem and feel it, too. The term *hitlabshut* figuratively expressed the rebbe's action in cloaking himself in the garment of the hasid's own thoughts, words, and deeds. These the rebbe examined from within, thereby fulfilling the Talmudic command, "Do not judge a man until you have arrived at his place." Taking this command literally, the rebbe assumed the place of the hasid and entered his consciousness. At the same time, though, the rebbe had to retain a strong hold on his own emotions and outlook.

In this unique process, the rebbe was expected to "become" the hasid for the moment. *Hitlabshut* was more than sympathy; the rebbe had already received the *kvittel* and thereupon seen the hasid in his personal essence, bare of all artifice. With this understanding, the rebbe could proceed to obtain the external information he needed to offer his guidance.

As Rabbi Joseph Isaac Schneersohn reported, "When the men of the covenant [i.e., hasidim] enter into *yehidut* and reveal the things that plague their hearts in their innermost being . . . then each thing they tell me I must find in myself in its subtle form. . . . Only then can one give an *ezah* and a *tiqun* ["rectification"]."

This process was not an easy one for even the adept rebbe.

At the moment when he was most intensely involved, he might suddenly feel the urge to flee the encounter and seek refuge in solitary study and prayer. But the rebbe knew that he could not escape his sacred responsibility; it was central to his purpose on earth. His master had shown him this. Yet, each time the rebbe opened himself to the hasid in *yehidut*, pain surged through him.

"I feel his pain even more than he does," Rabbi Nachman of Bratslav said of a hasid. "He can at least become distracted from his pain. I cannot." Therein lay the rebbe's problem. He had to consciously and deliberately enter the dark realm of his hasid's suffering.

What gave rebbes the strength to continue though often tired in such exhausting work? Many explicitly commented that the *yehidut* transported them closer to the Holy One. Paradoxically, they reported, in their most intense involvements with hasidim and their mundane difficulties, the magnificent splendor of the divine world became more real. In essence, one realm made the other possible.

Many Hasidic tales speak precisely to this crucial point. We are told that Rabbi Naftali of Ropshitz, always fond of joking and punning, one day in his later years decided not to speak anymore. His family was very much upset. They addressed him, but would receive no answer from him. Finally, they sent for his son, Rabbi Eliezer of Dzhikov, to see what was wrong with his father. Rabbi Naftali thereupon explained:

"At one time, in *yehidut*, I was able to keep two things in my mind simultaneously. I would joke with a person, while, at the same moment, direct very high unifications to the mind of God. Now that I am old, I am able to think only one thought at a time. I do not wish to speak, because to do so would mean that I cannot be in the presence of God."

METHODS OF AWAKENING

In readying his hasid for the *ezah* or action-directive, the rebbe possessed many techniques at his disposal. His training under his own master had taught him how to awaken the forces of inner growth. Knowing that his prescription would lose much of its power without the hasid's active involvement, the rebbe had to insure that his advice would be heeded. His array of methods was large; for our purposes, we will highlight those of catharsis and confession, shock and restructuring, arrangement-making, and dream analysis. No matter how these approaches differed from one another, they all flowed from a selfless love and caring. And, in all instances, the rebbe adopted his technique to fit the individual's particular needs.

Letting Go of Pain

One of the basic forms of emotional aid given to the hasid during *yehidut* was the encouragement of a cathartic release. The rebbe's goal was clear: to induce his hasid to let out suppressed pain; typically, feelings of sadness would well up in tears. Hasidic leaders taught that unexpressed emotions of guilt or sorrow over one's past misdeeds can lead to a repetition of the destructive behavior: one remains burdened with all his amassed regrets. Judaism had for millenia incorporated this notion; indeed, as far back as the time of the Temple of Jerusalem, worshippers confessed before the priest as he brought the sacrifice to God. The Hasidic founders translated this situation into the terms of the *yehidut*.

Often, the hasid was unable to connect his weeping during the session to any specific content or context of the dialogue. According to the rebbe, the hasid cried because "the spark had approached the Luminary," because the "cut-off limb" had regained its feeling and connection—and finally begun to experience the pain. Whatever the hasid's particular explanation for his tears, the fact remained that he cried. Seasoned hasidim would tell the novice that one who did *not* weep during such moments lacked in soul. In coming to the rebbe, the hasid sought to mend his soul; hence, his tears, they explained.

Because of the implicit rules of this sacred encounter, the rebbe would not console the hasid in his weeping; it would dissipate without the rebbe's help. However, the hasid sometimes found himself unable to cry in his master's presence. For a variety of reasons, this situation might have arisen. Perhaps, the hasid no longer felt his sense of crisis so acutely anymore. Or, the hasid might have become temporarily buoyed and elated by his delightful meetings with fellow hasidim at the rebbe's court. The young hasid sometimes felt overwhelmed and awed by the older, holy faces around him, and therefore, he was too numb to feel his own troubles.

Generally, the rebbe did not attempt to force a catharsis during the *yehidut*; he pitied those unable to release their pent-up emotions. Occasionally, though, the rebbe would sigh and even weep with the hasid. Such a move was sure to awaken some response from the hasid. When the rebbe wept upon reading the list of a person's misdeeds, and pitied the sinner's soul—"How low has he fallen!"—this induced many a hasid to weeping.

But even if the hasid had restrained himself during the encounter, he had other opportunities to let out his constricted feelings. The encouragement of his fellow hasidim, coupled with his own heightened expectations, typically allowed him soon afterwards to burst into tears, or to express himself in dance. In the early years of the movement, Lubavitch hasidim would dance the *mahol* after a counseling session with the rebbe. With this powerful method, the hasid would dance and weep simultaneously, as the whirling rhythms of the music carried him to new realms of wholeness.

The hasid danced the *mahol* with his eyes closed; lost in the outpouring of his emotions, he would punctuate the occasional phrase with an intense cry, or with the stamping of his foot. In later times, the Lubavitch hasid might simply seek a secluded corner to give vent to his feelings. But even this expected reaction was sometimes delayed, until the hasid had the chance to celebrate at the next major prayer session or *farbrengen*.

The first prayer session after he left the *yehidut* afforded one opportunity for delayed, inner release. Having been attuned to a particular outlook by the rebbe's words, the hasid listened with "new ears" to each syllable of the liturgy; sudden flashes of hidden meaning and inspiration might therefore appear. Any one of a host of liturgical phrases could personally speak to the hasid and spark his catharsis. Furthermore, because hasidim were expected to pray with fervor, the individual could really feel free to pour out to God all that he had previously suppressed.

While most hasidim experienced their emotional unburdening either during or immediately after the *yehidut*, some required a larger audience and setting—as well as the stimulation of alcohol and song. The *farbrengen* served this purpose. In the rebbe's absence, the *mashpiyah* was the main speaker. He might directly question a hasid about the *yehidut*; or initiate such discussion by recounting a counseling session of his own. The teacher's goal was not to embarrass the hasid, but rather to celebrate publicly the rebbe's virtues. "But for the rebbe, where would I be today?" often served as an opening gambit.

After a hefty drink of liquor, the hasid might join in a "heart melody," and at last, relate his own story—why he had come to the rebbe, what he had written on the *kvittel*, and so forth. From here onward, the hasid enacted the *yehidut*. When he reached the point of the rebbe's questions, advice, and finally, the blessing, the hasid might suddenly give way to his suppressed feelings—with sobs and weeping.

If all previous occasions failed to awaken the hasid's catharsis, he might find that a seemingly chance word, either at home or at work, would serve as the catalyst. Hasidim believed that each person can act as a divine emissary and that "coincidences" do not really exist. An apparently irrelevant comment might therefore provoke the necessary insight and emotional outpouring.

We are told that Rabbi Jacob Joseph of Polnoye left his counseling session with the Besht without committing himself to the Hasidic way. On his journey home, the Polnoyer passed a man on the road who asked for help to extricate his wagon from a muddy ditch. The Polnoyer replied, "I cannot help you."

To this, the man retorted, "No, it is not that you cannot help. You will not." Instantly, the Polnoyer understood what he had not wanted to face before and became a devoted advocate for the Baal Shem Tov.

Confession

Jewish tradition had historically allowed persons to confess before a sage; in some cases, too, the rabbinical court met during the month of Ellul to help penitents confess their sins. Nevertheless, the Hasidic founders did not require or institute confession on a regular basis. Rather, they heard confessions only when they felt that a particular individual might benefit from it.

In fact, Rabbi Nachman of Bratslav was the only Hasidic Master who incorporated confession into his standard method of counseling. He invited hasidim to confess their sins to him. Yet, he also encouraged them to pray in their own words—in addition to the regular services—and thereby pour out their innermost feelings to the Holy One. Rabbi Nachman recommended that each hasid spend time outdoors alone with God, and in this way, confess whatever was troubling one's soul.

Though few rebbes actually relied on confession as a regular feature of *yehidut*, some made use of it as a means to extinguish obsessive-compulsive behaviors. For instance, Rabbi Shalom of Belz once counseled a young man who found himself assailed by intruding sexual thoughts. The rebbe advised him to reveal every one of his upsettings thoughts to him. With much weeping, the young man did as he was told, and was never again plagued by this difficulty.

Such intriguing guidance derived from the Hasidic notion that obsessive-compulsive problems are often bound up with intense guilt and shame. The Hasidic founders taught that the suffering person feels overwhelmed by the recurrent invasion of his mind by obsessive thoughts. By confessing these to the rebbe or others, the hasid was seen to rid himself of the entire syndrome. For having shared the troubling thought with another, the hasid no longer felt dominated by its power borne of secrecy and shame. If an evil thought reoccurred, the hasid could then treat it lightly, even laugh at it.

The matter of timing was a crucial one in Hasidic counseling, especially so in hearing confession. The rebbe typically sought to insure that his hasid did not confess prematurely. Grief, shame, and guilt were all seen to play their part in sensitizing people to the need for personal change. In this sense, such emotions were regarded as having their useful functions.

Timing had still another purpose; any important insight one gained in the realm of mystical knowledge was to be kept secret for nine months, according to Rabbi Pinhas of Koretz. Only after this "gestation" would it survive as a viable form. Rebbes similarly cautioned against prematurely announcing a secret resolution for change; thus, it was not uncommon for a rebbe to rebuke his hasid for reporting or confessing a new, inner resolve that had not yet ripened into consistent action.

Hasidim who withheld from their rebbes especially holy and spiritual attainments were a source of much joy to their masters when the latter were surprised by these. The Great

Maggid took great delight when he learned in a roundabout way that young Schneur Zalman had twice been vouchsafed celestial meetings with the Prophet Elijah.

The Ruse of Identification

To penetrate the hasid's inner defenses, the rebbe sometimes adopted temporarily the hasid's outlook on his predicament. That is, the rebbe would seemingly agree with the hasid's definition of the problem, in order to enhance communication between them and accelerate the healing process. Such an approach was in direct contrast to their normal relationship, for the hasid was expected to identify completely with his master's perspective on life. Among the great Hasidic leaders, Rabbi Elimelekh of Lizensk and Rabbi Zussya took to confessing and weeping over the sins of their hosts, thus moving them to "turning."

Another means of caring and empathy is related in the following vivid story. A hasid once came to Rabbi Elimelekh to confess a capital sin. The rebbe advised him that he must atone for his sin by allowing himself to be executed in the ancient manner prescribed by Torah—by fire. This meant that the hasid would die by having hot lead poured down his throat. So great was the hasid's remorse that he was ready to brave this death. Rabbi Elimelekh, however, explained that the execution could not be carried out until the man had gone through the process of confession and penitence.

After the hasid completed the regimen of *teshuvah*, the rebbe called the hasid before others who were to be witnesses to his execution. Thereupon, the rebbe poured not hot lead down the hasid's throat, but honey.

The hasid protested vehemently that he really wished to be executed, but the rebbe pointed out that when a person has attained all the necessary levels of *teshuvah*, it makes no difference whether he receives lead or honey. Then the hasid

Rabbi Isaac ruled for the woman: within a year's time, the men were to repay her in full.

After she had left, the two men exclaimed to the rebbe, "Why do you believe such a slut? Her husband has been dead for over a year and people are gossiping that she is pregnant!"

Thereupon, the rebbe took hold of his beard and thoughtfully replied, "In that case, she will be in very great need in the near future. Go and pay her immediately what you owe her!"

The extent to which shock was used in the *yehidut* depended on the rebbe's personal style in confrontation, as well as his orientation and particular training. For instance, those of the Kotzk school employed shock more than their Chabad or Ruzhiner counterparts. Indeed, Kotzk hasidim viewed shock as a vital part of their treatment for inner difficulties. "I need a rebbe who will flay the living skin from my flesh, not one who will flatter me!" declared Rabbi Isaac Meir of Ger.

Restructuring

Another way to awaken the hasid's insight into his condition was to restructure his social situation. This placed him in a new vantage point from which to reexamine his habitual way-of-life. With the authority vested in their position, rebbes often shifted the social roles of their hasidim to effect these changes; the forces of some daily routines can blind people to their true paths, Hasidic leaders taught.

For example, Rabbi Schneur Zalman of Liady instructed Rabbi Joseph of Byeshenkowich, "For the sake of your soul, it is better for you to become a coachman than a rabbi." Such was Rabbi Joseph's initiation into the subtleties of guiding other souls. When he had completed this process of training and gained insight into his own character, the "coachman" was advised to become a teacher. This second shift occurred only after Rabbi Joseph had proven himself in a crisis, by bringing an errant Jew to *teshuvah.*

Sometimes, rebbes recommended temporary role changes for two purposes: to develop powers of empathy and to encourage new insights. To give their hasidim a fresh outlook, rebbes often insisted on the command of hospitality. They felt that one who becomes a host may be forced by rude or uncouth guests to accommodate himself to their pace and behavior. In so doing, the hasid would gain the opportunity to see life from a different point of view and thereby garner special insights.

The rebbe on occasion would counsel a hasid to live in exile. This too represented a temporary, though drastic, role change. Wandering incognito, the penitent-pilgrim virtually had to "kill" his persona, cast off his name, and wearing clothes inappropriate to his situation and manner, learn to develop his capacity for empathy and compassion. For this reason, such exile was seen to possess definite benefits.

Legend has it that even the Baal Shem Tov had to undergo this radical social change. After he became known, he was led to spend a Sabbath in the home of a seemingly uncouth person. In reality, the man was a hidden saint who wished to help the Besht avert a harsh decree that had fallen on him.

Hasidic literature is filled with many other examples of changes in role. We are told that a stingy man who had become very wealthy came to the Maggid of Mezritch for a blessing. Known for his selfishness, the man boasted that despite his wealth, he continued to eat only the simplest foods. Thereupon, the Maggid advised him to begin immediately to eat the richest and most expensive foods. The hasidim who heard this counsel could not understand it.

The Maggid explained, "When this man starts to consume and enjoy lavish dishes, he will see how stingy he has been. Thereby, he will also understand the plight of the poor, who have only bread and salt. But so long as he limits himself to eat only bread and salt, he will think that the poor can subsist on rocks."

Arrangement Making

Another important aspect of the rebbe's role as counselor lay in arrangement making. This interesting method was designed to free the hasid from the cross tug of tensions that bound him to inertia and fear of change. The technique did not depend on the hasid's understanding of what was occurring; rather, it involved a restructuring of his loyalties, duties, and priorities.

Nor did the arrangement need to represent a final action-directive for the hasid. It was sufficient that it merely divert the tensions restricting his upward momentum. In this way, he could finally marshall the energy to act decisively in order to grow.

The ruse of arrangement making was at times psychologically necessary because the person in need could not alter his precarious inner balance by himself. He typically felt too anxious to attempt any dramatic change; his emotional foundations were too weak to allow new inner construction—related, say, to his livelihood or family life—to be erected. He feared that his whole coping structure would subsequently collapse.

Thus, the rebbe's first move was to help the hasid shore up his defenses. The rebbe accomplished this by subtly distracting the hasid from overconcern with his present predicament—where, at tremendous emotional cost, he was on guard at all times. In this case, the rebbe's task was not as difficult as we might imagine, for he wielded tremendous status in the hasid's eyes. With so much faith in his master, the hasid was usually able to let down his defenses; at that point, the rebbe could more easily deflect him from his anxious preoccupations.

Then, step-by-step, the rebbe would induce a series of temporary insights until the Hasid gained a more "objective" insight into his situation. Thereupon, he felt secure enough to act without tension on the advice that the rebbe had intended from the beginning. The inner cramp that had held him immobile was gone.

This evocative process we have described is the one referred to by Rabbi Nachman of Bratslav when he discussed the method of helping those weaker souls whom he called "eggs." He explained that because their outer barriers are so weak, they can easily crack. Figuratively speaking, such "eggs" have both a blunted and a pointed end—representing insensitivity and sensitivity respectively, he taught. To help such a troubled soul, the rebbe had to "turn" him so that his "sharp end" was directed to appropriate realms of sensitivity and his "blunted end" to those areas where sensitivity was undesirable.

Regarding such souls as quite fragile, rebbes sought to "turn" them only gradually. In fact, Rabbi Nachman stated that one reason why the Messiah had not yet come was that the *zaddikim* wished to redeem even those weak souls called "eggs"—and that this process could not be hastened.

Dream Interpretation

For our examination here, the rebbe's last technique for awakening his hasid lay in dreamwork. When a hasid brought a dream for the rebbe to interpret, it was usually because of its disturbing content. Hasidim did not consider dreams to be mere folly; in keeping with centuries of Kabbalistic teaching, they viewed them as important and worth serious attention. Some types of dreams were viewed as messages—premonitions or warnings. If the dream troubled the hasid, he needed the rebbe's reassurance of its harmless nature, or else his active aid in counteracting the foreshadowing of future difficulty.

Hasidim believed that dreams had varying significance. For example, recurring erotic dreams were brought to the rebbe's scrutiny. These necessitated *teshuvah*, or penitence, for two reasons: first, because Jewish Law required a reparative act to redeem wasted semen, and second, because a dream

at night was attributed to waking thoughts. Since early
Hasidism generally sanctified sex within an early marriage,
there was little fuss about erotic dreams per se. The rebbe's
chief concern lay in the hasid's preoccupation with the dream
and his related feelings of guilt or anxiety.

In Talmudic times, Jewish leaders often sought to influence the physical and spiritual realms to avert ominous decrees from dreams. But the Hasidic founders adopted a very
different approach. Many decades before Freud's bold explor-
ations into the hidden workings of the psyche, rebbe and
hasid together sifted through dream material to understand
what it represented in terms of *hirhurey d'yoma*—the thoughts
and desires of the day. To do this, the rebbe strove to sort out
the jumble of images and symbols in the hasid's dream. These
were described as emanations from the world of *tohu* or "chaos,"
yet possessing their own logic and coherence.

A hasid once wrote to the modern-day Rabbi Joseph Isaac
Schneersohn and related a dream in which they spoke together.
The Lubavitch Rebbe responded, "The dream is caused by
the thoughts of the day. As one thinks by day, so one dreams
by night. . . . [Even] . . . if it is a good and proper dream, it is
only a dream."

Reb Ahre Dokshitzer, a Chabad hasid, came to Rabbi
Menachem Mendel I of Lubavitch and asked what one must
do to "grow in *Hasidut*." Rabbi Menachem Mendel replied,
"Study each discourse well and meditate on it sixty times.
What a person thinks of during the day he dreams of at night.
When does a person grow? When he sleeps. Study and you
will dream *Hasidut* and thus grow in it."

In another anecdote, when Reb Ahre Dokshitzer became an
old man, his daughter once came to wake him for synagogue
services. He resented being wakened from his contemplative
dream, but his daughter exclaimed, "Father, today you must
do it. Tomorrow, the time of reward, is time enough for
dreaming of visions."

Once the hasid had opened himself to change, the rebbe
expected him to accept responsibility for personal growth. To

aid the hasid, the *mashpiyah* and *haver* were always available. Sometimes, the rebbe would write a note on the *kvittel* and return it to the hasid. Back in his home surroundings, the hasid would reread such a note each night before going to sleep. At the same time, he would review his day's activities for evidence of his new, emerging Self.

The hasid knew that, at some later date, he would return for another counseling session. In their next *yehidut*, the rebbe would expect him to report on the progress he had made since their last encounter—and how the hasid had acted on his previous insights. With this foreshadowing in mind, the hasid strove for self-improvement in a deliberate manner.

In short, the key principle behind all of Hasidic guidance was that everyday life is the realm for inner growth. Rebbes utilized a variety of techniques to sensitize their hasidim to their need for a renewed way of life. In this way, they would be receptive to specific prescriptions for action. It is to this final state of the *yehidut* that we now turn.

CHAPTER SIX

REMEDIES OF ACTION

A woman once sent her mute son with a note to Rabbi
Menachem Mendel I of Lubavitch, that he help her find her absconded husband. Rabbi Menachem Mendel asked the boy a question,
and when he did not answer, commanded him, "Speak!" The boy
did so. Thereupon, the rebbe instructed him to tell his mother to go
to a particular town for the fair, and there she would find her
husband.

When the woman's son came out and told her what the rebbe had
said, she fainted with joy. The hasidim reported to Rabbi Menachem
Mendel that he had helped the woman not only by finding her
husband, but also by healing her mute son.

"Why doesn't anyone tell me these things?" he quipped.

—Hasidic oral tradition

HAVING LOOKED AT THE BROAD FEATURES of the *yehidut* and
how the rebbe diagnosed the problem before him, we turn
now to the specific forms of guidance he gave. For, ultimately,
the hasid came to his master for a prescription for action and
a new direction. Hasidim called this stage in the *yehidut*
encounter the *ezah*, meaning advice or counsel. The term was

also a cognate of the Hebrew root-word *ez* or tree; Hasidic imagery portrayed the *ezah* as a method by which the rebbe directs a hasid, just as an expert gardener turns or bends a tree for more fruitful growth. Thus, Rabbi Nachman of Bratslav described the rebbe as the "master of the orchard."

In the *shtetl* world of Eastern Europe, hasidim considered the *ezah* to be more valuable than even prophecy. They often insisted that a prophet can only foretell what is destined to happen; one capable of a true *ezah* can also *make* the event happen. Indeed, the results of the *ezah* often appeared startling and miraculous; the less it could be rationally explained, the greater seemed its divine power.

To the hasidim who venerated their rebbe, his *ezah* carried with it the authority of a fiat. Even if one thought that the rebbe might have misdiagnosed the situation and that his counsel was off the target, he was nevertheless to be obeyed in unquestioning faith. Because of Hasidic trust in the rebbe, his guidance was not supposed to be spurned once the *ezah* had been pronounced. If a hasid superceded such trust by trying to reopen the discussion, the rebbe vigorously discouraged or even forbade such a move by saying, "Let him [the hasid] not think that one [the rebbe] answers because he thinks this or that. One answers the way in which things are."

Hasidic tales abound which emphasized the secret wisdom of the rebbe's *ezah*, its capacity to transcend ordinary logic. Hasidim were therefore warned not to evaluate the guidance through common sense criteria—and that an apparently nonsensical piece of advice, based on the rebbe's seeming misperception of reality, would nevertheless lead to a triumphant resolution of one's conflict. Again and again, these stories would affirm that the rebbe had actually penetrated to a *higher* order of reality—going beyond the bounds of time, space, and causality.

For instance, we are told that a woman who sought the rebbe's help in locating her absconded husband was advised, much to her amazement, simply to go and do her marketing in a neighboring village. Following the rebbe's instructions, she

went to the marketplace, and there she found her husband.
Such unexpected and apparently miraculous forms of assistance were known as *moftim* or "signs." They were seen to
operate independently of the hasid's intellect and rely instead on his willingness to heed the rebbe's guidance.

In another tale, a hasid was in anguish over the fact that he
was to go on trial in a neighboring town. His rebbe gave him
the following *ezah*, "If one is to be put on trial, it is only
fitting that he travel there by first class." The hasid could not
see how this advice would benefit him, but did as he was told
and purchased a first-class train ticket. Once on the train, he
began to weep profusely. When a kindly man who was sitting
beside him asked why he was weeping, the hasid poured out
his tale. As it turned out, the man was the judge who was to
try the hasid's case and was himself on his way to the place of
the trial. After listening to the hasid, the judge instructed
him that when the trial began, he was to act as if they had
never met, and all would be well.

In other situations, the rebbe's *ezah* derived from insights
more accessible to the rational mind. For example, in order to
break or redirect a hasid's habitual style of behavior, the
rebbe at times would advise him to conduct himself in a new
or unfamiliar way. In this manner, the individual might be
able to throw off the blinders of habit and see the world
through fresh eyes. Thus, in "The Etzah," by Isaac Bashevis
Singer, a quick-tempered man is instructed by Rabbi Chazkele
of Kuzmir to act like a flatterer, not become one. Although
the man initially protests, he complies with the rebbe's request.
In so doing, the man restructures his personality and gains
inner wholeness.

In another tale, a hasid was in severe debt to his *poritz* or
landlord. Fearing imminent imprisonment for failure to pay
the rent on schedule, the hasid repeatedly came in tattered
rags to the landlord, to demonstrate his poverty and plead for
more time. The *poritz* remained obstinate. When the hasid
came to the rebbe, he advised him to wear his best, finest
clothes and speak with the confidence of the wealthy. Need-
less to say, the *ezah* worked. The hasid's posture of affluence

convinced the landlord that the man would be able to pay him.

In some instances, the rebbe had to take into account a hasid's fickleness or tendency to contradict authority figures. "Reverse psychology" was therefore employed. Deliberately, the rebbe would steer such a "buck" in the wrong direction, so that he would unknowingly find himself on the proper course. Such reverse psychology could also serve the hasid when he had no access to his rebbe. For such a situation, Rabbi Bunam of Pshiskha suggested, "How did Abraham know how to act before the Torah was given? He questioned the idolaters of his day. Whatever they said, he did the opposite." Likewise, a popular Hasidic joke of the time was that when in doubt as to how to behave, "ask a *Mitnagged* [Hasidic opponent] for his advice, and then do the opposite." Generally, though, rebbes were hesitant to make use of reverse psychology for its manipulative quality and attendant dangers.

Interestingly, they often counseled the practice of charity as a prelude to the experience of a mystical *mofet*; the more heroic and selfless the act of giving, the greater and more powerful was deemed the hasid's merit. For this reason, the rebbe hoped to awaken the hasid's sense of charity in such a way that he would act on his own initiative; if the rebbe had to demand that the hasid behave charitably, such a prescription was seen to detract from the merit of the act. Sometimes, the rebbe might advise a hasid in financial straits to *give away* his last, remaining savings. Although the hasid might feel that this action would only worsen his predicament, the rebbe would insist on its execution. As was only known to the rebbe, the man's wealth would thereby be doubled through a divine *mofet*.

Despite his exalted reputation, the rebbe typically refused to take credit for the success of his *ezah*. Like Rabbi Pinhas of Koretz, he would say, quoting Bahia, "When a man conducts himself properly, he can see with an eye that is not an eye and hear with an ear that is not an ear. Therefore, when a hasid comes to ask an *ezah*, I hear how he himself tells me to answer him." In short, Rabbi Pinhas taught that the hasid's problem contained its own solution. With the proper empathy, the rebbe could find the answer hidden within the other's being.

When the rebbe knew of no other means by which to prepare the way for a necessary "sign" to alleviate the hasid's distress, he would advise the recital of psalms. This prescription followed millenia of Jewish tradition; as the psalter had written, "He who wants to soften the rigors of God, let him tell all his praise [i.e., recite all the psalms]." Rabbi Pinhas of Koretz concisely recommended, "For all kinds of conditions, recite the entire Book of Psalms without a break." But, the Hasidic leaders stressed, these had to be pronounced with intense devotion—as though King David himself were addressing them to the hasid—to be effective.

Ultimately, the hasid's faith in the rebbe and the Almighty was the key toward his accepting the *ezah* as a transrational prescription for action. If the hasid truly believed that through sacred prayer—such as at the graveside of a *zaddik*—his situation could be altered, then the miraculous could occur. After all, the *Zohar* had clearly stated, "If it were not for the prayers of the righteous [in the World to Come], this world could not exist for half an hour."

Sometimes rebbes advised that the hasid take a bit of earth from the grave of a *zaddik*; legend has it that during a raging epidemic, hasidim were helped immediately, when they sowed into their garments small packets of holy earth from the grave of Rabbi Dov Baer of Lubavitch. But Rabbi Pinhas of Koretz observed that an even more powerful act of faith exists. "When great trouble befalls a person," he wrote, "then he should do nothing save trust in the Lord. He should not take medicine, or pray, or go to the *mikveh*, but simply trust truthfully, and by this means will his salvation come."

In the sections to follow, we will therefore examine some of the major types of Hasidic advice given to those seeking help. In particular, we will look at the important realms of physical and mental health, marriage and family, and livelihood. We will conclude with the rebbe's blessing, the final stage of this lofty encounter, the *yehidut*.

HEALING THE INFIRM

In the Hasidic world, physical health was esteemed as vital to one's ability to serve God fully. Rebbes denegrated self-punishment and exhorted their followers to pay heed to their physical well-being. "Good health is as important a positive commandment as donning phylacteries," was the popular saying. Similarly, the Maggid of Mezritch warned that, "When a small damage occurs in the body, a large damage results in the soul." Thus, rebbes readily offered their assistance to those seeking relief or cure from physical ailments.

The Hasidic founders typically adopted a multifaceted approach to disease. Ultimately, they attributed all illness to the will of God; if an *ezah* was to help in any way, it had to be directed toward the end, "May it be His will that. . . ." Yet, the Besht and his adherents also taught that man has the freedom to choose and that most sickness results from an emotional or spiritual imbalance. Indeed, the early Hasidic literature is replete with insights into the link between mind and body. Other aspects of Hasidic healing, though, such as the use of amulets, indicate that we cannot ascribe their practices solely to objective concepts.

To the Hasidic founders, a sick person's "will to live" was a key element in his ability to become well again. They knew that without this desire, no intervention could truly be effective. Thus, each rebbe had his own particular method of awakening the ailing hasid's motivation to health. The Baal Shem Tov once quoted the Talmud to a learned man, asking him, "Do you enjoy pain?" The man replied in the Talmud's words, "Neither suffering nor its beneficial effects." In short, by appealing to the hasid in a familiar idiom—and provoking an answer that the other knew—the Besht was able to stimulate the man's will to live. Building on the libidinal yearning for life, Rabbi Nachman of Bratslav required an ailing hasid to recite the Canticle.

Interestingly, the Kobriner condemned histrionic healing scenes and argued that to dramatize a person's illness only strengthened it. His counsel to the sick, therefore, was, "No signs! No stormy prayers! A little Torah and a roll and milk is all you need." Another rebbe advised an ill colleague who had lost his will to live, "Sure, you can die and be in heaven, and this you will enjoy. But isn't it better to live and give God joy here? Get well!"

These are but a few examples of the *ezot* that rebbes prescribed to accentuate the hasid's desire for well-being. In keeping with the *ezah*'s intent, such prescriptions were aimed not at the hasid's symptoms, but at the source of his difficulty: namely, his loss of the will to live. The rebbe insisted that only when this quality had been rejuvenated could the manifest illness begin to improve.

Consistent with their emphasis on the nonphysical aspects of health and sickness, rebbes made use of the power of suggestion in healing. Indeed, according to Hasidic tradition, the universe is filled with suggestions. The heavens proclaim the glory of God and the earth contains countless secret hints. Every creature is a reflection of some higher, supernal being. The rebbe reinforced this outlook through his gestures and often purposely ambivalent speech, intended to point to many levels of reality at once.

Sometimes, the rebbe noticed that the hasid clung to his illness from inner guilt and an unconscious desire for self-punishment. Therefore, by provoking a cathartic confession and emotional release, the rebbe freed the hasid to accept the blessing, and ultimately, a return to vitality. Thus, the blessing itself was a form of suggestion that strengthened the rebbe's advice during the earlier stages of the *yehidut*.

The more sophisticated the hasid, the more he felt the need to adapt the rebbe's suggestion to his own outlook about bodily

health. To assist the hasid and increase his suggestibility, the
rebbe often accompanied his blessing with a "word" from the
Torah. In so doing, he elevated his blessing to a higher level
in the hasid's eyes. For instance, a woman once came to her
rebbe because she was suffering from an abnormal discharge.
He assured her that she would be well, then added from the
Torah, "Before the Lord, you will be purified." The woman
understood this remark to signify that she would be purified
of her unclean flow.

It should be noted, though, that only rarely did the rebbe
actually resort to what one might assume to be intense, post-
hypnotic suggestion in his work. For, to involve the hasid in a
new course of action, his conscious and intentional participation was necessary. The fundamental belief was—at least
among Chabad hasidim—that each person must attain his
own inner rungs.

Usually, the rebbe's assurance that "All will be well," or
that "God will send you a speedy recovery," satisfied the
hasid's need. However, if the rebbe saw that the hasid craved
something tangible as evidence of the blessing's potency, he
might also receive a *s'gulah*. A Kabbalistic term, *s'gulah* referred to a charm that, because of deeply hidden correlations,
had a power that was ascribed to transcendent forces. The
word *s'gulah* also designated the power that the charm was
seen to radiate.

In medieval times, Kabbalists related the *s'gulah* to zodiacal
influences; among the hasidim, though, the rebbe's charismatic power was regarded as its driving force. Most hasidim
trusted in the rebbe's inner strength far more than in any
external object, no matter how exotic. Rebbes utilized their
own names in making amulets. We are told that the Baal
Shem Tov thus revised the earlier practice of inscribing in
the *s'gulah* a name of an angel or of God. Rabbi Moshe Leib of
Sassove simply wrote the word *shabbat* ("Sabbath") on his
amulets and trusted in this power to insure its effectiveness.

For the rebbe whose view of man derived from a soul-body
interaction, the purpose of the *s'gulah* was to help neither the
soul nor body in isolation; *s'gulot* were designed to facilitate

their interrelation, or to treat physical symptoms through
their moral concomitants. Though we can readily see the
possible placebo effect s'gulot might have exerted, some Hasidic tales do not lend themselves to this interpretation. For
example, legend has it that some persons in a coma or thought
dead were healed through imbibing a potion of the rebbe's
wine.

Generally, s'gulot exuded an intense symbolic significance,
as rebbes employed substances related to Jewish sacramental
life. Such materials included scraps of matzoh, etrog, wine, oil
from Sabbath lamps, Sabbath foods, and haroset (the Passover
halvah paste, reminiscent of the "mortar"). S'gulot also ranged
from herbal medicines and symptomatic palliatives to occasional coprophiliac substances.

Whenever s'gulot pertained to the Torah, they were ascribed special power due to their spiritual significance. Among
Hasidic leaders who conducted healings, those who practiced
"Torah signification" predominated. For instance, the daughter of the Belzer Rebbe once advised a man suffering from a
painful leg cramp to give a box of candles to the synagogue.
Later, when her father asked why she had prescribed this
measure, she quoted from Torah, "A lamp onto my feet . . . is
Thy Word." In another story, a rebbe called a person with
gangrene to the Torah and read to him, "Thy foot did not
swell," and the man was healed.

The Hasidic founders emphasized that the rebbe's personal
power was necessary for the s'gulah to be effective; upon his
demise, it was seen to lose its potency. In a relevant and
humorous tale that has come down to us, a woman with
frequent headaches sought the help of Rabbi Menachem Mendel I of Lubavitch; he recommended that she bathe her head
in hot water each time a headache approached. She did so
and was cured. However, when Rabbi Menachem Mendel
died, the trusted method failed to work. Thereupon, she followed the counsel of his son and successor Rabbi Shmuel of
Lubavitch, who advised her to try cold water instead. And
this too worked. But, when Rabbi Shmuel passed on, his cure
no longer helped. When her husband came to Rabbi Shalom

Dov Baer of Lubavitch, the next rebbe, he smiled and suggested, "Why doesn't she try mixing the hot and cold water together?"

Yet another intriguing Hasidic approach to healing was through touch and laying-on-of-hands. Some rebbes relied heavily on this method to treat physical illness. We are told that Rabbi Shalom of Belz once attributed the healing power of his fingers to their involvement in Torah study. Rabbi Nachman of Bratslav taught healing based on subtle diagnoses of bodily pulse. He reported that he experienced energy depletion each time he engaged in laying-on-of-hands. Perhaps because of this common effect, not every rebbe wanted physical contact with his hasidim.

When rebbes employed the healing touch, they usually included a *lahash*, or whispered blessing. Unfortunately, only scant information has survived on this practice. It seems that the rebbe would sometimes pronounce the name of an ascended rebbe, as an accompaniment to his physical manipulations of the hasid's body.

While the early hasidim readily carried out such exotic healing methods, they were far more ambivalent about using orthodox medical techniques. In fact, two rather distinct attitudes existed on this subject. Certain rebbes felt that hasidim need not place their faith in secular forms of care and that reliance on medication was therefore unnecessary. These rebbes insisted that all that one needed was to remember, "I, the Lord, am your healer." This outlook, of course, has been been similarly advanced by numerous religious groups.

Other rebbes recommended the use of medicinal substances. For example, Rabbi Barukh of Medzyboz argued that into bitter materials God had placed healing properties, so that their divine sparks could be raised and redeemed. When the Besht's granddaughter lay sick, he sent his daughter the following advice, "Take a teaspoon of good oil and put it in a glass. Mix some white ginger into it, adding a jigger of brandy and some soap. Let this mixture sit for two hours and then rub the child's feet before sleep, and this will help." This prescription was clearly for an analgesic rub.

Legend also has it that, centuries before penicillin was

developed, the Baal Shem Tov would scrape off the mold from rotting cheese and rub it in one's wound for effective healing. In the nineteenth and twentieth centuries, a few rebbes even studied pharmacology or medicine. Some without formal training, such as the Piasetznoer, wrote prescriptions that were honored by practicing pharmacists.

Of course, this sort of intervention presupposed the rebbe's ability to make an accurate diagnosis without the benefit of medical instruments or tests. Hasidim often told one another stories of their rebbe's capacity to discern illness and pre-scribe the corrective remedy. Such anecdotes closely parallel the reports that flourished about Edgar Cayce and other fa-mous seers and clairvoyants. In some cases, the rebbe found it necessary to contradict the physician whom the hasid had consulted. The rebbe would enter the conflict by quoting the Baal Shem Tov, "You looked at the sick man from the physi-cal side, and I from the [more comprehensive] spiritual one."

We are told that the modern-day Rabbi Joseph Isaac Schneer-sohn once sent a woman to a famous surgeon for a thorough evaluation. The rebbe gave her a note to give him. Intending first to test the doctor, she did not do so until after he had examined her and pronounced her well. Thereupon, the sur-geon read the note, which identified the presence of a maligant tumor. He again examined her and found the rebbe's impres-sion correct. Surgery was then arranged and proved success-ful in removing the malignancy.

Sometimes, the rebbe did not refer the hasid directly to a particular physician, but indicated only the place to seek medical aid. "Travel to . . . and there you will find help," the rebbe might say. Since this vague counsel was often offered in nonmedical situations, the hasid did not regard it as strange. Indeed, guidance of this nature was designed to test the hasid's faith; he was not supposed to press for more specific information, but follow diligently the rebbe's directives as given. Later, upon returning from a successful mission, the hasid would tell his peers of the rebbe's miraculous vision.

Similar to treating other problem areas in the hasid's life, the rebbe might refer a medically difficult case to a colleague, perhaps one more skilled or "specialized" in this domain. Legend has it that a young man with tuberculosis visited several rebbes to no avail. Finally, he was helped when he visited Rabbi Pinhas of Koretz, who prayed that the man be given an ample livelihood. "Having opened the gates of sustenance," Rabbi Pinhas commented, "I managed to sneak in and open for him the gates of healing, too."

The rebbe's aid as a healer extended not only to the grave, but beyond it as well. When he knew that a hasid's illness was terminal, the rebbe provided guidance as to how to meet death. He counseled on such relevant subjects as one's attitude toward leaving this life, dying in a lucid and serene state, and preparing for further growth in the World to Come.

However, the rebbe did not merely offer abstract advice on such weighty matters; he served as an outstanding model in his own behavior. As Chapter 1 of this book indicates, many Hasidic leaders died with their full faculties intact and employed their remaining moments on earth to teach the mysteries of the transition. They cautioned their followers not to fear bodily death, but to welcome it as a necessary stage in one's inner development.

For this reason, rebbes would often impart hints of their approaching end, so that their hasidim could observe their preparations for leaving this existence. Later, disciples would regale one another with tales of their master's departure. When the Squerer heard that his brother, the Chernobiler, could no longer don phylacteries, he knew that the Chernobiler's end had come. "A *zaddik*," the Squerer thereupon observed, "dies willingly when he can no longer fulfill any *mitzvot*."

Visiting a dying hasid, Rabbi Nachman of Bratslav advised him, "What? Worries over death? There is a much nicer world there!" In saying this, he helped the Hasid accept his fate with serenity. The man was assured of a better world beyond this realm. Another story tells how Rabbi Nachman offered to teach a hasid how to die—on the condition that the man would return after death to report how it went. Indeed, the hasid facing death was often comforted by the rebbe's promise to aid him even after his earthly demise. Such reas-

surances were possible since both rebbe and hasid believed in
the availability of after-death assistance. By asking the hasid
to come to him afterwards for further counsel, the rebbe
provided comfort that death was simply a state of transition.

Following a hasid's demise, the rebbe consoled the bereaved.
To the grieving family, he offered such words as, "Your son
already hears Torah in heaven"; "Be glad you were a foster
parent to so holy a soul"; or "If you knew how the one you
mourn lives and mocks your weeping, you'd stop." The
Chernobiler comforted a rebbe's son by saying, "Your father
now teaches in heaven." Besides providing consolation, the
rebbe also advised families as to proper burial and mourning
procedures.

Hasidim strongly believed that after their bodily death, the
rebbe would mend and elevate their souls to loftier realms.
Because they had given him a sacred *pidyon*, they knew he
would fulfill his obligations to them. Thus, when one rebbe
voiced that he did not wish to aid a deceased one, another
disciple rebuked him, "Either you help him, or you won't be
my rebbe!" We are told that Rabbi Nachman continued to
guide a baker after his death; he had often furnished breads
and cakes for the hasidim.

Like other Hasidic leaders, Rabbi Nachman fully expected
his disciples to come for counsel even after their earthly
demise. Legend has it that he and a disciple were once making plans for the High Holy Days. Discussing those who
would be attending his services, Rabbi Nachman asked, "And
how about Moshe? We haven't heard from him."

The disciple replied, "Rebbe, Moshe died several months
ago."

Vividly expressing the Hasidic viewpoint, Rabbi Nachman
answered, "So, just because he died, does that mean he can't
come for Rosh Hashonah?"

In short, rebbes dealt with physical illness and its aftermath
as a basic aspect of their calling. To them, bodily discomfort
was no isolated phenomenon, but a condition intertwined with
one's emotional and spiritual state. But how did they treat mental disease? It is to this intriguing subject that we turn next.

SOOTHING THE TROUBLED SOUL

Similar to their multitiered approach to physical illness, the Hasidic founders expressed varying views toward mental disorder: that is, cases in which people repeatedly and grossly violated religious and community norms. One master intriguingly argued that the normal human condition is insanity and that only by the grace of God are individuals sane. Another espoused that madness is a disease of the will. Rabbi Aaron of Karlin articulated the notion that "There is no mental illness without pride. . . . All mental illness is based on wanting to have one's own way."

Yet other rebbes taught that emotional sickness, like its bodily counterpart, derives from the evil inclination: when people sin, they make themselves vulnerable to the "spirit of folly," which can then seize hold and turn them from moral behavior. From this perspective, mental illness represents a fall from consciousness or "right knowing"—a state of profound forgetfulness of one's higher nature.

Certainly, one of the most prevalent forms of emotional distress within *shtetl* life was depression. Even a casual perusal of early Hasidic sermons and tracts reveals that rebbes were very much concerned with identifying and treating this debilitating condition. From the unrelieved economic and political hardships of Jews in that milieu, it is hardly surprising that many people fell prey to feelings of hopelessness and despair; powerlessness and self-doubt easily become chronic and pathological. Rather, what is difficult to explain is that such energetic, optimistic figures as the Hasidic leaders even existed—promulgating a message of joy when so little outwardly justified it. The Besht had repeatedly urged, "There is a great rule in the service of the Creator: guard yourself from sadness in every possible way."

It is important to note that the Hasidic founders focused specifically on the real, clinical signs of depression and not on normal reactions to the vicissitudes of life, such as grief and mourning. Anticipating modern psychology by centuries, rebbes like Nachman of Bratslav and Schneur Zalman of Liady pinpointed such behavioral signs as listlessness and lethargy, loss of appetite and sleeplessness, and the inability to shed tears as indicators of serious depression. Conversely, if the rebbe felt that the hasid was merely trying to avoid confronting his appropriate emotions of sadness, he would be made to face these.

Two basic methods existed by which rebbes treated depression; sometimes, these were used together. With the first, the rebbe sought to arouse the hasid's sense of excitement and anticipation of gratification, such as from spiritual sources. Occasionally, the hasid might also be permitted to regress to more physical pleasures, provided these were sanctioned within Jewish and Hasidic practice.

The second approach—known as the *bitush* or "shattering"— was predicated upon the rebbe's belief that chronic depression can best be broken by heightening the condition to a piercingly acute state. Interpreting the story of Exodus on this level, they taught that the hasid must sacrifice the lamb— his "animal soul"—in order to liberate his imprisoned yearnings for renewed life.

How was this "death" to be accomplished? Sometimes, the hasid's discipline was intensified through fasting and enforced solitude. But above all, rebbes strove to induce the hasid to cry—not with fleeting tears, but with wracking, soul-wrenching sobs, weeping that welled up from one's entire being. Feelings of aching dullness had to give way to release. The hasid's inner resignation was transformed first to the worldless scream, "Help me, Father!"; then to a long, long wail like a *Shofar* blast; then to a broken weeping; and finally, to a shattered wimpering. Only after utter despair could come laughter and joy, the Hasidic leaders stressed.

The hopelessness that had characterized the inescapability of death had become the impetus for a flight to life.

Of course, not every person was strong enough to withstand such a crisis; but the rebbes regarded palliatives and easy assurances as serving ultimately only to prolong a serious depression. As long as one appeared able to withstand the *bitush*, no one could spare him the ordeal. It was deemed the surest and quickest way to mental recovery.

Another common type of emotional disturbance among *shtetl* folk was what we would term hysteria. In essence, hysteric manifestations result from inner conflict and take the form of dramatic impairment or paralysis of the muscular-sensory system. For instance, a woman may suddenly find that she cannot move her hand or leg; one morning, a man may awaken blind or mute. Such cases were far from rare among East European Jews of the time; in fact, they formed the initial basis for Sigmund Freud's private practice in Vienna about a century later.

Generally, rebbes seemed to have treated hysteric episodes as though they were real, physical illnesses. In a sense, rebbes assisted the sufferer by accepting his symptoms as legitimate, but yet banishing these without shaming him by suggesting that he had been feigning true sickness. In this way, the hasid had little motive to adopt new symptoms, as he had gained special, community status as "one who had been healed." His desire for attention having been satisfied, he no longer felt it necessary to cling to his disorder. He could return to normal life.

Thus, rebbes were often called upon to help women in difficult labor to have normal deliveries. Under intense anxiety and fear, they were tightening their own muscles and thereby increasing their agony. A gentle, soothing word from the rebbe, or an amulet with the "name" on it, frequently succeeded in calming the woman in labor and effecting a smooth delivery.

So it was with the blind, the lame, and the mute. In one dramatic instance, the rebbe restored a man's sight, then withdrew it. The rebbe wanted to show that he had the power to heal the man, but he did not deserve it. We are told that a rebbe once said in a deaf-mute's presence, "Drown him, shock him, wake his nerves!" and this alone was sufficient to heal him. In another tale, the rebbe first restored a man's hearing and then helped his speech.

Sometimes, the rebbe demanded a certain sacrifice on the part of the hasid's family before agreeing to effect the cure; perhaps, the Hasidic masters were more knowledgeable about subtle, family dynamics and "sick roles" than we think. For example, the father of a deaf-mute son was asked to promise no longer to shave. Because of the intense social sanction involved, this oath represented a real sacrifice on the father's part. Only after he himself had completely accepted the rebbe's condition did the boy's cure take place.

From our present-day vantage point, obsessive-compulsive behavior was also common in the *shtetl*. Some hasidim were afflicted with a sense of perpetual anxiety and guilt concerning the fulfillment of religious obligations. They felt in need of guidance, to learn how to conduct themselves more meticulously. Some, no doubt, anticipated approval for their zealousness. Such persons were usually in for a rude awakening when they went for their *yehidut*.

Rebbes generally regarded over-scrupulosity as a symptom of emotional imbalance. They expected their hasidim to observe the Jewish Law with selfless delight, not with grim determination or boastful self-congratulation. On this subject, the Stephaneshter poetically remarked, "Scrupulosity is a cloak made of pride, lined with anger, and sewn with melancholia."

In a modern Hasidic story, a rebbe once rebuked his prideful colleagues at a rabbinical convention. As they preened themselves on their zealous religious observances, he suddenly announced his own scrupulous refusal henceforth to eat yellow cucumbers. When his colleagues pressed him for an explanation, he sardonically replied, "Why? Because they taste bitter to me."

By denying the hasid the satisfaction of obsessive-compulsive conduct, the rebbe was often able to shock him into a more modest and ultimately more harmonious lifestyle. Certain

Hasidic groups, though, viewed such an aberration less seriously than did others.

Certainly, no examination of *shtetl* mental illness and its treatment would be complete without a look at the *dybbuk* phenomenon. Of course, from the Hasidic perspective, possession of one's being by an invading psychic entity was a grave spiritual disorder, not primarily a sign of emotional imbalance. Such an invasion was seen to have been the result of a vulnerability due to some inner, moral lapse on the individual's part. They believed that such a person had become "weakened" by his unholy thoughts or deeds, thus opening himself to the *dybbuk*'s power.

There were several behavioral signs that suggested to rebbes that the individual was possessed. These included a marked loss of appetite and the will to live, severe introversion, and occasionally, convulsions. When urged to eat or behave normally, the person might turn abusive and hostile, sometimes shaming family members in public. He might hurl lurid insults at others, or show contempt for holy rituals or objects. At times, he might unexpectedly regain his ordinary personality for brief periods and complain of being controlled by another being. Eventually, the family would take the sufferer to the rebbe.

Hasidic exorcisms were typically community affairs. Before assembled hasidim who served as witnesses, the rebbe would speak directly to the offending spirit, rather than to the sufferer's normal self. The rebbe would ask questions as to its identity and origins: invariably, the *dybbuk* would reveal itself as a discarnate soul who had committed some horrible sin in earthly existence. As divine retribution, it had been condemned to wander in the void.

Finally, the rebbe would order the *dybbuk* to depart; if it initially refused, the rebbe issued dire threats of eternal wandering or offers for later healing and uplifting. At times, the rebbe might even ask a *dybbuk* how it might be helped. Thereupon, the entity was perceived to leave—and the person restored to health. Once again, the rebbe's transcendent knowledge and power had triumphed over the forces of darkness.

MARRIAGE AND CHILDREN: FORMS OF COUNSEL

While Jewish family life in Eastern Europe has often been romanticized and portrayed in idealized colors, strains and tensions certainly existed. It was a world far different from ours. Marriages were usually arranged for men and women— often still in their mid-teens. Couples bore many children, in the hopes that some might survive to adulthood. Most people lived within walking distance of relatives and in-laws; several generations frequently shared the same household. Solitude and privacy were almost nonexistent; each sex had distinct and separate religious and social duties to perform.

To be sure, Hasidic leaders celebrated the virtues of a pious Jewish home. They extolled the merit of a relaxed and peaceful family life, and the love between husband and wife. Echoing the sacred teachings of the *Zohar*, rebbes preached on the sanctity of the marital union and its reflection of the heavenly bond between the King and the *Shekinah*. Indeed, one who had not yet married was seen as spiritually incomplete, unwhole. As the *Zohar* had tersely stated, "A man who is not married is defective and the holiness of the King flees from him."

Nevertheless, the reality of Hasidic family life was far from idyllic. Some of the major rebbes served as poor models in this domain. Many were more accessible to their followers than to their own families. Some Hasidic leaders and their adherents, busily building up the movement, spent weeks or months away from their wives and children. In fact, the great love relationship in Hasidic literature was between the rebbe and his hasid.

Yet, exceptions existed throughout the Hasidic tradition. Some rebbes showed such kindness and devotion to their family members that they inspired many of their followers to do likewise. The Baal Shem Tov hoped that he and his spouse would ascend to heaven in a whirlwind. But when the Besht's wife died, he declared, "I thought that a storm would sweep me up like Elijah to heaven. But now I am only a half a body, and this is no longer possible."

Generally, men came to the rebbe for marital advice only in cases of severe conflict. Husbands harbored few expectations of exuberant, romantic excitement in their marriages; they hoped for warmth, stability, and an uncompromising respect for their spiritual responsibilities. Unless one's situation at home had become truly unbearable, the man was advised to place his religious obligations before his familial ones. Rabbi Shalom Dov Baer of Lubavitch thus advised, "The wife is screaming? Let her scream. The child is screaming? Let him scream. He won't die from screaming. . . . do what the Most High demands."

Rebbes sometimes sought to improve the husband's attitude about the noise or lack of privacy in his household. The classic Yiddish folktale of the man who complained of overcrowding at home speaks to this theme in Hasidic counseling. According to the story, the rebbe first advises the man to bring into house one barnyard animal after another, until he can scarcely breathe from the stench and noise. Thereupon, over a period of weeks, the man is allowed to withdraw each animal, one at a time. Finally, the home is as before, but now, the man can hardly believe the spaciousness of his quarters.

In many instances, the rebbe interpreted the man's marital problems as having a spiritual purpose. To one henpecked husband, the rebbe counseled that God had decreed the marriage from above to teach him the virtue of patience. To another man, embroiled in miserable and bitter wedlock, his rebbe explained that the Heavenly Tribunal had arranged the marriage in order for him to atone for sins he had committed in his previous existence. Jewish mystics had long taught that every marriage is the result of divine plan: man and woman are placed together for their mutual, proper inner development. Rebbes therefore rarely advised a couple in conflict to divorce.

Nevertheless, in accordance with Jewish tradition, rebbes recognized that sometimes irreconcilable differences between husband and wife necessitated this drastic act.

Cases of abandoned wives were far from uncommon in the *shtetl* culture. These unfortunate women hoped that the rebbe could find their absconded mates. The woman's plight was far greater than that of the man whose wife had forsaken him; he could obtain a decree signed by one hundred rabbis, setting aside the ban against polygamy. But it was legally impossible for a woman to obtain a divorce without her husband's consent.

For this reason, the rebbe's task was largely to provide reassurance and to indicate where she might locate her husband. Rather than describing the specific place, though, the rebbe characteristically referred the woman to its general vicinity. He might say, "Go, now, to the town of . . . and there you will find your husband." Hasidim would celebrate the mysterious manner in which the rebbe's advice worked; however, he tended to downplay its miraculous nature and attribute it to common sense.

Since the couple rarely became reconciled once the husband was found, he usually could be persuaded to release his wife from the marriage contract. Legend has it that Rabbi Menachem Mendel of Lubavitch refused to receive women for *yehidut* until his wife declared that her prolonged illness resulted from his attitude on this matter. From that time on, Rabbi Menachem Mendel counseled both men and women.

In the *shtetl* world, barrenness was associated with death. To have no one to recite the Kaddish after one had died, was to lack even the assurance of eventual liberation from suffering. Who could help the barren? Didn't Sarah of the Bible conceive by miraculous intervention and didn't the Shunamite woman conceive upon Elisha's sacred promise? For the hasid, only one person could aid, and he was the rebbe. Hasidim journeyed hundred of miles to receive his blessing for children.

For the most part, though, rebbes did not consider their blessing sufficient to insure conception. They compared the blessing to the watering of a plant—necessary but useless unless the seed had first been sown. They therefore prescribed a variety of *s'gulot* to help the couple overcome barrenness. Typically, these avoided the whole issue of biological infertility and its physiological correction. Nor did rebbes ordinarily ask intimate questions about the regularity of the wife's period or the timing of the husband's ejaculation.

However, there were some exceptions to this rule. The rebbe might ask the hasid whether he followed the Talmudic prescriptions to eat fish for its stimulation of semen production and garlic for its libidinal effects. The rebbe might also advise the hasid to take cold water baths for sixty days if he suffered from premature ejaculation; rainwater was suggested as an aphrodisiac. Rabbi Naftali of Ropshitz recommended that if the woman experienced irregular menstruation, her husband should maintain a consistent schedule of intercourse with her.

S'gulot for barrenness tended to focus on magical-religious determinants. For example, hospitality was the primary injunction to insure fertility, since it showed to God that one could take care of others. In this view, children do not "belong" to their parents but rather are temporarily entrusted to them. Rebbes pointed to the Biblical stories of how the hospitality of Abraham and the Shunamite woman had in each case directly led to being blessed with offspring. Hasidim also believed that Elijah himself had tested the hospitality of the Besht's father, before he was blessed with a child.

To insure that the wife would conceive, the rebbe often suggested various measures to bring her and the husband into harmony on the transcendent plane. Sometimes, barrenness was ascribed to the couple's lack of *shalom bayit* (peace in the home). In opposite cases, the rebbe might advise that they should not strive for too much togetherness. Legend has it that when a childless couple came to Rabbi Barukh of Medzyboz, he advised that they immediately obtain a divorce. After personally supervising its administration, he called the couple back and said, "Now, get married again. This time I will conduct the wedding and you will have children."

Rabbi Barukh then explained to the astonished couple the reason for this maneuver; he thereby shed light on the spiritual interpretation of the significance of the marriage ceremony. The rebbe recounted that, at the time of their wedding, they had failed to undergo the proper ritual in which the bride surrounds the groom seven times. Since man is basically polygamous, it is necessary that the bride surround her groom seven times to be like seven wives unto him, Rabbi Barukh commented. Because the couple had omitted this ritual, the husband had not become completely bound to his wife and female succubi thereupon adhered to him, robbing his semen of potency. Now that the divorce and remarriage had been effected, Rabbi Barukh was able to promise the couple children.

Sometimes, rebbes advised Hasidic couples on what to do to facilitate the woman's pregnancy after she had conceived. For example, Rabbi Elimelekh recommended that every Saturday night she should eat something for the sake of the "Sabbath Queen" and declare that this was being done. In cases of difficult delivery, the rebbe offered his intercession and a s'gulah to aid the mother. His advice to the husband encompassed such diverse realms as acts of charity, special prayers, and vigils by the grave of one whose merit might redeem the woman from her suffering.

"In order that [hasidim] not exert themselves in emptiness, nor give birth to tumult," rebbes also provided s'gulot for infant survival. Indeed, in the early days of Hasidism, infant mortality was rampant and a pervasive condition of shtetl life. Hasidim sought the rebbe's help in this domain, for they remembered the Biblical story of the Shunamite woman who had brought her ailing son to Elisha's private bedchamber. With the Prophet's divine assistance, the child had fully recovered.

In one intriguing tale, a father whose children had all died in infancy came to the rebbe for aid. The anguished man used the Yiddish phrase, literally translated, that his youngsters had failed to "hold on." Since the hasid was clean-shaven, the rebbe advised him to grow a beard, so that his children would have "something to hold onto." Following this counsel, the hasid was overjoyed to find that all his children born thereafter survived.

Hasidim sought their rebbe's help too with all phases of child rearing, particularly those relating to initiation into stages of Jewish duty. The rebbe would offer his guidance on such diverse matters as the child's naming and weaning, the first cutting of his hair at three years of age, and his entry into study and observance of the Law.

Those children who, either due to ancestry or their outstanding behavior, possessed a special destiny in the Hasidic community received particular attention from the rebbe. Sometimes, the parents of such a child requested the rebbe's presence at the circumcision ceremony—to insure the child's sexual virtue. Rabbi Nachman of Bratslav attracted many parents with his promise, "Any child brought to me before the age of seven will not sin before marriage." Indeed, the rebbe served as both sponsor and guarantor of the child's moral life: for this reason, he often cut the child's first lock of hair, or in a few special instances, personally taught him the beginning Hebrew alphabet.

When parents experienced difficulty in child rearing, they anxiously sought the rebbe's assistance. They became extremely distressed if their child seemed to stray from the traditional Jewish way—and turn instead to the lures of the "Enlightenment" or Christianity. If the child appeared attracted to another Hasidic group, that, too, was cause for alarm. Thus, the parents looked to the rebbe for support and advice.

In some cases, the rebellious child was summoned to the rebbe, who would speak with him directly. In other instances, the rebbe might offer various suggestions to the parents so that they might act as his "deputies" to help the youngster. Occasionally, the rebbe felt that the parents themselves needed to be rebuked for a lifestyle that had created the child's misdirection.

ADVICE FOR ECONOMIC AND POLITICAL SURVIVAL

Hasidim often sought the rebbe's guidance in matters relating to livelihood and political protection. They respected his wisdom and ability to see beyond the mundane into the higher realities surrounding everyday life. Knowing that the Baal Shem Tov had emphasized the importance of seemingly ordinary activities, hasidim were not ashamed to ask for help in coping with vocational, financial, and governmental problems. They had to bear in mind, though, that these realms were all subordinate to the hidden workings of the Almighty.

When coming to the rebbe for vocational guidance, the hasid was not interested in his personal aptitudes or interests. Rather, he desired a livelihood that would help him fulfill his purpose on earth, his particular mission in uplifting the fallen sparks of existence. He therefore expected the rebbe to use his intuitive powers to counsel him correctly. For as the present Lubavitch leader, Rabbi Menachem Schneersohn has observed, "When the *yezer hara* ("evil urge") seeks to dissuade one from his work . . . it seduces the soul to do what belongs to another."

Rebbes taught that those who avoid their special tasks in life are "errant souls." The contemplative who engages in extroverted activity, the scholar who takes on philanthropic duties, the wealthy merchant who refuses to aid the needy— all are straying from their true path. Rabbi Nachman of Bratslav stressed that to change recklessly one's central task to another leads to an embittered life. One's ardor soon cools, however initially exuberant. Thereupon, the person becomes inwardly blocked, unable to conduct either his own task or his assumed one. Further incarnations might then have to be endured, Rabbi Nachman indicated.

Sometimes, though, a hasid might have already completed his mission on earth. He might sense genuine urges for some new challenge to undertake. In such instances, the rebbe would help him by offering a new direction and emphasizing that "a wise man does not have to wait for his next incarnation: he can begin again in this life." In so doing, the hasid felt he was changing his luck—his source of energy inflow from above—and generating abundance for himself and others.

The rebbe's vocational advice often transcended mundane logic; he counseled based on what he saw as the hasid's life-task. In one tale, Rabbi Israel, the Maggid of Kozhenitz, once reluctantly advised a hasid that his task was to become a thief, a master burglar. The hasid did not understand the counsel, but he had no choice but to comply. Only later, when the man had achieved the purpose of his earthly existence through his work as a thief, did he comprehend. After making full restitution, he settled down to an honest life.

At times, rebbes even viewed poverty as a desirable means to spur a hasid's inner progress. Some rebbes discouraged their hasidim from amassing great wealth—"Go back and face your poverty in God's service" was often the counsel. Yet, rebbes also stressed that the wealthy are meant to "serve God in other ways than faith and trust." Once again, the rebbe treated each hasid in a manner appropriate to him.

Often the rebbe's vocational guidance dealt not so much with the choice of livelihood as with the manner in which the hasid pursued it. Legend has it that a man who worked as an entertainer at weddings complained of his poor income to Rabbi Pinhas of Koretz. His advice was, "Keep yourself from telling jokes when you are not getting paid for them, and you will make a better living." He explained this counsel as follows: "It is written that a person's income is budgeted from *Rosh Hashonah* to *Rosh Hashonah*. It doesn't say that his food is budgeted, but that his enjoyment is budgeted. Since you derive so much enjoyment from the jokes you tell, you are cutting off your own income."

From the sixteenth through the mid-nineteenth centuries in Eastern Europe the *poritz* or landlord loomed as the symbol

of State authority over Jews. Even those with adequate liveli-
hoods often found themselves dangerously behind in their
rent payments. *Pritzim* (plural) were wealthy landowners, the
landed gentry. They typically placed great demands on their
Jewish tenants, who were viewed as neither serfs nor free
persons. Rural landowners frequently boasted to one another
of the loyalty and cleverness of "their" particular Jews, deri-
sively called "Moshke" as an ethnic label. However, the really wise one was not "Moshke" but his rebbe, who guided
him through his economic straits.

There seems to be no uniform pattern by which rebbes
advised hasidim how to deal with their landlords. Sometimes,
the rebbe would recommend that the hasid play the role of a
nebish, a poor nitwit, to avoid persecution. In other instances
the rebbe advised a more aggressive, proud posture. If no help
were available to the hasid without the funds for rent, he was
incarcerated in prison.

In such unpleasant circumstances, rebbes often assumed
the responsibility of raising the necessary ransom money.
One of their favorite methods to accomplish this was first to
tell a group of hasidim a story illustrating the spiritual reward for heroic generosity, and then, offer them a share in
the great *mitzvah* of ransoming the captive Jew. Certain rebbes roamed the countryside to carry out such vital work.
Rabbi Moshe Leib of Sassov became renowned for making it
his chief mission in life.

Jews in the *shtetl* were bewildered by a government they
could not comprehend. For Jews to believe that the same
government that sanctioned pogroms and persecution—and
relegated them to economic subservience—was also the guarantor of law and order was impossible. The Jew who saw a
brass button knew only one thing: if the official would "take,"
he was a good one; if incorruptible, he was also untrustworthy.
One who could be bribed was deemed at least human. By
their meager salary and bureaucratic load, officials were virtually condemned to accept bribes. Such was the political cli-
mate surrounding the rebbe and his hasidim.

Thus, East European Jews widely believed that military

service was not an occupation for them. "By thy sword thou shalt live," was, after all, the Biblical heritage of Esau. Most *shtetl* folk felt strongly that to defend a country in which they were manifestly in exile hardly justified a single drop of their blood. For this reason, hasidim turned to their rebbe for guidance in avoiding conscription. He, in turn, actively collaborated in helping them stay out of military involvement.

Hasidim usually petitioned the rebbe by saying, "Rebbe, my son has to go for his physical tomorrow. Please pray that he be found unfit." The rebbe might then ironically bless the youth, "Be well and healthy. But in their eyes may you appear sick." Or, he might boldly advise, "I see no reason for you to appear at the physical. Run away and cross the border." In other instances, though, the rebbe would caution the young man, "Go and serve. You are well and it will not harm you. Later, you will survive because of this training."

The rebbe's methods of assistance were often quite resourceful. To fool the authorities, some rebbes advised the hasid to alter his name, or even secretly to adopt the identity of an exempted man who had recently died. While rebbes rarely counseled self-mutilation as a way to escape conscription, some hasidim deliberately cut off their trigger fingers; to have a hernia was a mark of distinction. Certain rebbes concocted special herbal potions so that the hasid would seem to suffer from a serious disease and therefore be deferred from service.

Once a hasid had been inducted, the rebbe would seek to meet with him and offer comfort. Some rebbes secretly rendezvoused to provide religious services to conscripted hasidim. Rabbi Israel Meir Hakohen wrote a compendium, *Mahaneh Israel* ("The Camp of Israel") to help Jewish soldiers cope with their many problems. He issued the famous dictum to sustain life in wartime conditions, "You may eat nonkosher meat. But you must not gnaw at the bones."

In the domain of taxes and travel visas rebbes had little practical advice to offer. The government made its own, unilateral decisions in both arenas; yet, in cases where the hasid feared complications, he sought the rebbe's help in the *yehidut.* Whenever he could suggest some concrete course of action, the rebbe did so. Such matters usually depended on the hasid's ability to make a favorable impression on the appropriate official. Therefore, the rebbe strove to awaken in the Hasid greater confidence; indeed, he believed that his master's blessing drew down a divine "thread of grace" to aid him.

In matters of pogroms and Jewish self-defense, rebbes operated in an unseen world. They directed their efforts mainly to the celestial "prince of the country" and its "guardian angel." Hasidim attributed all subsequent events on the physical plane to the rebbe's capacity to influence these supernal realms.

However, some rebbes participated in, or even initiated, political action to improve the security of East European Jewish communities. Of course, there was little room to maneuver in the autocratic and feudal structure that existed. Certain rebbes spearheaded petitionary delegations to the government and thereby fought for Jewish protection. Rabbi Shmuel of Lubavitch cleverly used the weapon of economic leverage against the czarist regime. To the minister of the interior, the sage daringly threatened to publicize abroad the czar's refusal heed the protest against ongoing pogroms. That way, foreign Jewish capitalists might take retaliatory measures. Enraged, the minister ordered the Hasidic leader arrested. But the rebbe did not alter his stance in the slightest. Seeing that its foreign image would suffer, the regime squelched the pogroms. Despite such incidents, though, there is scant evidence that rebbes actually prepared their hasidim for armed resistance or counterattack.

As to the issue of emigration, rebbes generally espoused either of two rather separate attitudes. Many of them yearned to settle in the Holy Land and breathe its exalted air; they dreamed of a new and better life beyond the *shtetl*. The Jewish spiritual homeland beckoned warmly to such figures. Some, like Rabbi Nachman of Bratslav, risked their very lives just to make a pilgrimage to the Holy Land. He commented thereafter that his real spiritual birth had occurred during that sacred visit. Other rebbes permanently relocated there, taking with them their entire "courts" and hundreds of followers.

Yet many other rebbes felt that God had placed them for a purpose in the diaspora, to serve His people with devotion and commitment. Few, therefore, advised their hasidim to move to the Holy Land. "Better a dry morsel of bread in the rebbe's company, then the fanciest meal far from him" was the popular adage.

In a beautiful Hasidic tale that illustrates this outlook, Rabbi Wolf Kitzes once felt an intense yearning to journey to Holy Land. He decided first to seek the counsel of the Baal Shem Tov. However, prior to the meeting, Rabbi Wolf Kitzes went to the *mikveh* and as he immersed, he beheld a vision of the Holy Temple. He entered the sanctuary and proceeded to the inner sanctum, the "holy of holies." There, he saw an empty space. Upon asking where the sacred ark and tablets were, Rabbi Kitzes heard the heavenly reply, "In Medzyboz with the Besht."

Rebbes often told this story in counseling those who wished to relocate to the Holy Land. In fact, many hasidim who had emigrated there from time to time consulted rebbes in Eastern Europe or elsewhere. For such hasidim knew that even the distance spanning continents was insignificant compared to the wisdom and guidance that a true spiritual master could bring. To encounter such a figure, hasidim were willing to challenge the very limits of time and space.

THE BLESSING

The last stage in the *yehidut* was the blessing. It could not come before the end of the session. It was the final seal. Just as a handshake finalized a business transaction, so too the blessing finalized the *yehidut*. The hasid had only to say

"Amen!" to it; he did not even need to hear it fully. "God has heard the blessing," and that is what counted.

Nevertheless, the blessing's power was attributed in part to the hasid's collaboration. He had to carry out diligently the rebbe's *ezah* for the celestial decree to be actualized. As Rabbi Menachem Schneerson observed, "A blessing needs something to take hold of. For example, the blessing of rain requires a ploughed and seeded field ... [otherwise] no use will come of it, no matter how much rain falls."

The blessing had other key functions. By pronouncing it, the rebbe thereby recharged the energy source within himself. The blessing also served to ratify the covenant between rebbe and hasid—as well as strengthen the relationships among the other hasidim involved with the particular *ezah*.

In most instances, *yehidut* blessings followed the formula of the liturgical devices for intercession. Many began with the words, "May God help that...," and then, as in the case of sickness, "... Moshe son of Sarah shall speedily be healed." Certain rebbes preferred long, detailed formulae that united the teaching word and the *ezah*. Some recited the formula while holding the hasid's hand; others placed their hands on the hasid's head. Still others pronounced the blessing without any physical contact at all.

Neither participant wished to trifle with the blessing, perhaps the most solemn moment of the entire *yehidut*. Some rebbes stood when bestowing the blessing; knowing how the hasid hung on its every word, they enunciated clearly. Other rebbes deliberately slurred the blessing, so that the hasid's simple faith in God be strengthened by the mystery of not hearing its precise content. Sometimes, the hasid might not comprehend the intent of a blessing which derived from foreknowledge not yet available to him, but already accessible to the rebbe.

Interestingly, some rebbes were noted for pronouncing apparent curses, both which later proved to be blessings. They explained their tactic as a ruse against Satan, who according to legend, sought to block a straightforward blessing, but not a seeming malediction. For example, Rabbi Zussya was known to bless Jewish children with the formula, "May you be healthy as a *goy!*" This utterance was explained as a ruse against Satan, who was seen to protect the Gentiles from harm.

The Zanzer Rebbe was famous for slapping some of his Hasidim at the time of the blessing. His followers told that if he slapped a hasid on his face, then help had already arrived. One man who came hoping to be blessed with children instinctively ducked the rebbe's blow. Realizing immediately what he had done, the man thereupon pleaded with the rebbe to slap him again. But it was too late.

Hasidim did not always wait patiently for the rebbe to bless them. Sometimes, the rebbe stated that he could not promise the requested boon—heaven seemed to offer no such blessing. In such cases, the hasid pressed the rebbe for further effort and a pledge that he would keep on trying. Imitating the rebbe's tactics when he verbalized to God, the hasid might insist, "I shall not leave this room, rebbe, unless you promise and bless." The rebbe accepted such seeming impertinence as permissible, since he had set the example in his own pleas to the Almighty. In fact, the rebbe made use in his prayers of the hasid's stubborness. "See, Lord, how they insist. And why? Because they want to serve You better. Do they not deserve to be helped?"

Another way to force the rebbe's blessing was to come upon him unawares. A person might ask him for one thing, when he actually sought another. The opening tale of this chapter—about the woman with the missing husband and mute son—illustrates this situation. In a similar manner, Rabbi Pinhas of Koretz was able to pray for sustenance when he could not promise health; having achieved sustenance for the hasid, Rabbi Pinhas next strove for the man's health. When the rebbe saw his hasidim use his own spiritual tactics on him, he rejoiced that they had learned so well.

Occasionally, the rebbe felt certain that there was no possible opening for imminent assistance and refused to succumb to the hasid's pleas; the supplicant would be forced to surrender to his lot. Some hasidim, though, rebelled against the rebbe's resignation and sought the aid of another master. At times, this approach seemed to work.

After having received the rebbe's blessing, the hasid would seek a secluded place where he could fix the *yehidut* firmly in his memory. Fellow hasidim would typically wish him *gut gepoyelt* (literally, "well achieved"). In some instances, as was the case in Rabbi Schneur Zalman's early ministry, the hasid was welcomed into a post-*yehidut* dance, the *mahol*. With the encounter's stress behind him, the hasid could let himself go, even into a celebrative ecstasy, and sing out his thanks to God for the rebbe's counsel and compassion. So important was the *yehidut* to the hasid—and this was especailly true for his first session—that "many hasidim counted the day on which they came to Lubavitch as their spiritual birthday."

Both rebbe and hasid left the *yehidut* with an "understanding," though one not always explicit. However, if the hasid's interpretation of the session differed greatly from the rebbe's, the *yehidut* had not been satisfactory: by definition, it implied that a mutual pact had been made. The rebbe realistically knew that the hasid's impression of what had transpired would not be identical to his; still, the rebbe hoped that their viewpoints were not too divergent.

Certainly, the *yehidut* had not terminated their relationship, but only reinforced it. According to Hasidic tradition, the rebbe would at times think of the hasid; if the latter were inwardly sensitive, he would feel this event at home. The rebbe's post*yehidut* obligations covered a wide range—from the promise that "He who touches my doorknob will not die without *teshuvah*," to making sure that the hasid actually received what the blessing proclaimed. The protective care of the hasid, the pledge to be with him during crises, and the promise to keep in touch psychically—all of these were implicit. At appropriate times, too, the rebbe would reread the hasid's *kvittel* and again intercede on his behalf.

The hasid's awareness of his own obligations was equally far-reaching. He vowed to carry out faithfully the rebbe's *ezah*, maintain his active association with other hasidim, study with his teacher, participate at *farbrengens*, contribute to the cause financially, and by mail report of his inner progress.

Rebbe and hasid usually did not prearrange for the next *yehidut*. It was by nature a "crisis" event and neither wished to anticipate another. The hasid might allude to upcoming plans to see the rebbe—say, on a particular Sabbath or holiday—so that the rebbe might mark the event with divine favor. He rarely stipulated a specific time to meet with the hasid again, except in the case of a disciple or trainee.

When groups of hasidim were about to leave the town of the rebbe's domicile, he often came to see them off. The hasidim then sang a *nigun*, which bespoke their sadness at leaving him and their desire—God willing—to commune once more. When traveling along the road to home, hasidim often met one another and spent an extra day en route, recounting all that they had heard and witnessed at the rebbe's court.

If the rebbe had come to a town away from his regular domicile, the hasidim would accompany him at his leavetaking. They sang *nigunim* expressing their sorrow at his departure. When the rebbe was ready to travel on at greater speed, he would stop the carriage, and with a final, parting blessing, take leave of his hasidim. Thus, the sacred convenant was sealed and renewed.

INTO THE LIGHT

THE WORLD of the *shtetl* is no more. What still remained in the twentieth century of the unique way-of-life we have described perished in the fires of the Holocaust, where thriving communities were reduced to ashes and lone survivors. No matter how nostalgic we may feel, *shtetl* life possessed a certain fragile innocence that seems impossible for us to ever fully recapture.

And yet, the legacy of Jewish, especially Hasidic, existence in Eastern Europe may prove far more enduring than many observers have previously guessed. It is astonishing—would "miraculous" be too strong a word?—to witness the growing excitement and influence that classic Hasidism and Kabbalah are once again exerting on Jews and non-Jews alike. Such persons are not only discovering a dazzling philosophical richness in the Jewish mystical tradition, they are also finding a lively, experiential pathway reaching to the Holy Source within us.

In this work, we have looked closely at the fascinating role of counseling in the Hasidic milieu. We have preferred to let the material speak for itself and have sought to keep interpretations to a minimum. The implications of Hasidic advice-giving for us today appear manifold, ranging from its lofty outlook to its practical methods for awakening our creative, intuitive potentials. As we have seen, the Hasidic founders were intimately acquainted with regions of consciousness—both lower and higher—that current, scientific explorers of the mind are just beginning to recognize and map in detail. In their ability to connect the ordinary, day-to-day problems of their hasidim with sacred realms, rebbes exhibited a clarity of purpose we can only strive to emulate in our own efforts to offer aid to those in need.

But for me, what is perhaps most striking about this provocative tradition is that, despite the vast authority that rebbes possessed in their culture, they did not expect to catalyze inner growth in their hasidim without the support of others. That is, with all of their exalted status and skill, rebbes relied on each hasid's special friend, teacher, and peers, to help spur one's personal advancement toward wholeness. No one was expected to develop emotional and spiritual strengths in isolation.

In a time when genuine rebbes seem scarce indeed, this feature of Hasidic life appears very relevant for our own situation. It is often easy to forget that others may act as guides and helpers. Such figures need not always wear the guise of rebbe; they are all around us.

To the extent that we can rekindle this quality of spiritual comradeship and community in our lives, the divine energy of early Hasidism may transform the mundane world once more. We may better sense the splendor behind our everyday acts, and thereby, truly elevate the sparks each of us has been entrusted to redeem.

Edward Hoffman

INTIMATE CONVERSATION
IN THE PRESENCE OF GOD

*Then did those who are in awe of God converse with one another—
and YHVH listened in and heard—and wrote it into His book of
re-member-ance before Him, entitled "Those who are in Awe of
God and value His Name."*

(Malachi 3:16)

SINCE I FIRST had a *yehidut* with the late Lubavitcher Rebbe,
Rabbi Joseph Isaac Schneersohn in 1941, I have been impressed by those wonderful occasions when, either as hasid or
rebbe, I have experienced this sacred dialogue. Each time, I
have been affected by the momentousness of such an encounter.
From the beginning, I have sensed that Martin Buber's description of the I-Thou relationship applies fully to the *yehidut*.
Yet, this quality is present not only when participants are in
the roles of rebbe and hasid. The specialness, the magic, the
truth and mirroring can happen sometimes with friends, at
other times with complete strangers.

People with whom we are not usually willing to relate in a
vulnerable and open way can engage us in a shattering *yehidut*.

174

Once, a stranger confronted me on a busy street. He challenged, "Are you sure?" and walked away.

Another person, drunk and staggering, walked up to me at a bustling intersection and asked me, "Is there such a thing as real?" He then continued, "How old are you?" When I, taken aback by his *hutzpah*, told him, he replied, "Does it pay to live that long?"

Such figures were Prophet Elijah in disguise, delivering messages that I needed at those moments. The child who was my rebbe by raising a naive and yet trenchant question, as well as the therapist who made me face my pain had too a real connection with the *yehidut*.

The *yehidut* is a process, and rebbe and hasid are the roles for two participants within it. There are times when the roles are unclear, despite the fact that they are formally structured. At times, I have felt that all the problems others raised with me were my own—at least on one level or another. My responses have been spoken not only to others, but also to myself. The Talmudic rabbis characterized this situation with their dictum, "Let your own ears hear what your mouth is saying."

In this process, one person's intuition enters into harmony with the intuition of the other. As body faces body, empathy attunes to and intertwines with empathy, mind addresses mind, and soul intuits soul, effects are created in the two destinies. In this way, people experience themselves as two cells of one organic being, parts of an hitherto unguessed, holy, whole, and divine gestalt. There is a flash of ephemeral knowing in search of words to capture the theophany of that here and now.

Those in other traditions, who have received darshan or mondo from guru, sheikh, lama, or roshi, have known the *yehidut* in different modes. Those who have had deep, heart-to-heart talks with friends, when all was open, those who have had peak experiences *à deux*, know the *yehidut* on some level.

The helping professional can benefit from moving into the "space" of the *yehidut*. The pastor, minister, priest, and rabbi can turn an interview into a *yehidut*. Some inner change to God-related intention is necessary, though. For to be a *yehidut*, it must bear the mark of the professional, of being karmicly nonpolluting; one must prudently judge what is for the "client/hasid's" best interest. The therapist, like the rebbe, must also possess the qualities associated with the term "amateur"—namely, a love for the process and a warmth and comradeship for a fellow God-wrestler.

One cannot take for granted that the "client" will be prepared for as deep, close-to-telepathic, a process as the hasid has with the rebbe. Such an encounter is often emotionally overwhelming, capable of flooding the client with stimuli he or she cannot handle. An inappropriate *yehidut* can produce anxiety, or even worse, paranoia and a "closing down"; it must not be attempted indiscriminately. One can misguidedly create dependency and a subtle—or not-so-subtle—bondage. The therapist who lacks the ascetic, liturgical, and spiritual tools of the rebbe—and who tries to step into the rebbe's shoes—may do more harm than good. This is why the question of one's focus and preparation needs to be addressed with care. The therapist/rebbe must be an adept in *Heshhon Hanefesh*, the examination of one's conscience and motives.

This is where we must begin to speak about *davvenology*. For there is more to Hasidic prayer than petitioning God and participating in public worship. There is a process in *davvenen* that takes the prescriptions of *Halacha* (Jewish Law) and embodies these as attunements to God's will. This psycho*halachic* process takes the rubrics and intentions of the Kabbalists and turns these into transformative experiences. It lives life in the context of the inner landscape where God is present.

In this process, the soul makes her transits through the stations of the yearly calendar and the passage of events in one's personal life. On this plane, God's purposes in history, messiah and salvation, death and reincarnation, are processed—just as they are in the reality-map of the hasidim.

The present day Hasidic establishment would not look kindly at the person who, not having been the scion of a Hasidic dynasty, would hang out a "rebbe" shingle. The standards of

that establishment are quite strict as regards *halachic* observance. Yet, even precise observance does not entitle a person
to serve as a Hasidic rebbe. The high rank and lofty social
position of rebbes tend to mark them as distancing, even
forbidding, archetypes. One who wishes to apprentice himself may have difficulty in finding a rebbe who would act as a
truly accessible model.

If the helper is a woman, the distance from a rebbe willing
to teach her is even greater. Hannah Rachel, the Maiden of
Ludmir, lived more than a century ago. She manifested all
the qualities of piety, learning, and charisma, with the added
mystique of teaching and counseling from behind a curtain
men who sought her guidance. Yet, she suffered persecution
from colleagues. There is an awakening today among women.
Some hear an insistent call to a pastoral ministry and it is
urgent that we have women rebbes.

Who can even guess what kind of "rebbe work" women
could do? History (Her Story?) tells us that since the time
when women were persecuted for their paranormal and charismatic gifts, we have lost much of our balance. As a result,
men have produced overweening and predatory technologies
that threaten to destroy us. Would it be too much to say that
what was special about the early Hasidic rebbe—and what
distinguished him from his rational-legal, *Mitnaggid* counterpart—was that his mode was more mothering than fathering?
Perhaps, it was this matriarchal function of the rebbe—
listening to problems, telling stories, healing with the heart—
that gave Hasidism its *shakti*-feminine-*wicca*-pervading power.

Such wisdom was never codified in books; it evolved and
developed by apprenticeship and attunement. It is not in its
nature to let itself become the subject of state board exami-
nations. It also calls on a vertical dimension that relates to
prayer, intercession, spiritual healing, and the power of
blessing. Training in that vertical dimension is not as readily
available, though, as the more horizontal process in workshops and growth groups.

It may not be easy to acquire the training necessary for
doing *yehidut* from today's heirs of the great Hasidic masters

of the past. But it is possible. If you are male and you are ready to take on the reality-map and lifestyle of the hasidim, you can contact Chabad-Lubavitch—for many, the most accessible Hasidic group. After a time, you may decide to choose some other Hasidic school, one closer to your intuitive and emotional outlook, and then continue your training.

Not everyone may be in the position to permit himself such a radical change in lifestyle. Yet, there is a way to synthesize the necessary diet—namely, the state-of-the-art psychological and psychospiritual growth technologies. These include such empirical techniques as Yoga, Taoism, Zen and Sufism, besides, of course, Hasidism. Among the teachers of these disciplines one might hope to acquire some of the process that makes for the *yehidut*.

The processes of *davvenen* are also the focus of my work with B'nai Or. We train people acquainted with the growth technologies to become familiar too with the methods of *davvenen*. For those who have worked in traditional *davvenen*, we provide bridges to holistic awareness. We thus have the possible beginnings of a school for the rebbes of the future. Their tasks will encompass all that the rebbes of old had to do and also to orchestrate collectivities of persons gathering sparks into holy and cooperating gestalts. In this way, we hope they will contribute to the process of peacemaking and planetary healing.

MAY HE WHO MAKES PEACE ON HIGH MAKE PEACE FOR US AND FOR ALL ISRAEL AND FOR ALL THE SOULS WHO FORM THE EMBODIMENT OF THE REBBE, THE SPIRIT OF GUIDANCE.

GLOSSARY

Ahavat Yis ra'el. Love of Israel, love of fellow Jews.

Avodah. Literally, "inner work, liturgy"; service of the heart, sacrament, sacrifice.

Ba'al Habayit. Literally, "House owner"; a full fledged member of the community.

Baal Shem Tov. "Bearer of the Good Name," the popular appellation of Israel ben Eliezer (c. 1698–1760), the charismatic Hasidic founder.

Besht. An abbreviation of the Hebrew name, "Baal Shem Tov."

Bitush. Literally, "chopping"; a rebuke administered by oneself or by others.

Bokher. A young, unmarried man.

B'yahid. Alone.

Chabad. The metaphysical system developed by Rabbi Schneur Zalman of Liady (1747–1812). The basis for Lubavitcher Hasidic thought, this term derives from the abbreviation of the first letters of the highest three *sefirot* or divine forces—*chochmah* (wisdom), *binah* (understanding), and *daath* (knowledge).

Daven, davvenen. (Yiddish) To pray or worship, live the liturgy, with bodily motion and chant.

Devekut. The inward state of cleaving to the divine.

Dybbuk. A discarnate spirit possessing the soul of a living person.

Ein Sof. The "Infinite," from which all forms in the universe are created.

Elterer Hasid. An older hasid.

179

Eynikl. (Yiddish) Grandson.

Ezah. Counsel or advice; the direction to be followed; the solution to the problem.

Farbrengen. (Yiddish) A session of Hasidic fellowship, at times presided over by the rebbe.

Gabbai. Overseer, secretary.

Gan Eden. Garden of Eden or "Delight"; paradise.

Gaon. Genius; title given to an exceptionally brilliant Talmudist.

Gehenna or *Gehennon.* Purgatory, where the soul is cleansed of earthly impurity.

Goyim. Literally, "nations or ethnics"; non-Jews.

Halacha. Literally, "the way to walk"; the legal system of Orthodox Judaism.

Halachic. Relating to *halacha.*

Hasidism. The popular, charismatic movement which arose among East European Jewry in the late eighteenth century. *Hasid* means "pious" in Hebrew; in twelfth-century Germany, an unrelated group was likewise known as the *hasidim.*

Hasidut. The teachings of Hasidism.

Haver. Friend.

Havurah. Friendship group, fellowship.

Hayah. In Kabbalistic terminology, the second highest realm of the soul.

Hazaquah. Legal term for holdings, possessions.

Heshbon Hanefesh. Literally, "figuring the bottom line of the soul"; the examination of conscience.

Hibut Haqever. Literally, the "beating of the grave"; state of purgation in the afterlife.

Hirhurey d'yoma. Daydream.

Hitbodehut. Literally, "self-isolation"; the practice of being alone with God; some form of meditation or private devotion is typically involved.

Hitlabshut. Investment.

Hitlahavut. The mental state of "burning enthusiasm" for the divine in all aspects of life.

Kavanah. The classic rabbinical term for mental concentration. Among the hasidim, *kavanah* came to be associated with the type of "one-pointedness" of intent necessary for higher states of awareness.

Kabbalah. From the Hebrew root-word "to receive." Often used as a generic term for Jewish mysticism per se, it more precisely refers to esoteric thought from the late twelfth century onward.

Kaf Haqela. The "catapult" phase of purgatory in the afterlife.

Kvittel. (Yiddish) A short note; a written request for aid which the supplicant presents to the rebbe.

Lahash. Literally, "whisper"; an incantation.

Ma'amarim. Formal discourses.

Maggid. A great spiritual master.

Mahol. A dance popular among early Lubavitch hasidim in which one danced with his eyes closed.

Mashpiyah. A Hasid's spiritual guide or tutor.

Maskilim. "Enlightened Ones," referring to the first assimilationists among Western Jews in the late eighteenth and early nineteenth centuries. The Maskilim were highly contemptuous of Kabbalistic and Hasidic elements of Judaism.

Mikveh. The ritual bath.

Minyan. A quorum of ten men together for public religious worship.

Mitnaggedim. Orthodox Jews who were "Opponents" of the Hasidic movement. The Mitnaggedim went to great lengths to attempt to supress the spread of Hasidism among East European Jewry.

Mitzvah, mitzvot (plural). A divine commandment; good deed.

Mofet, moftim (plural). Literally, a "sign" or miracle. In Hasidic parlance, a miracle performed by the rebbe in the service of his pastoral work.

Mokhiah. A chastizer or admonisher.

Moreh Derekh. Teacher of the Way; one who instructs in the divine path.

Nefesh. The lowest, most physical portion of the human Self. The nefesh dissolves upon physical mortality.

Neshamah. The nonphysical, transcendent part of the Self. The *neshamah* continues after bodily death; below *hayah* and *yehidah* in the hierarchy within the soul.

Nigun. A melody.

Pidyon. Literally, "ransom"; a sum of money given to the rebbe at the *yehidut.*

Pilpul. A form of Talmudic debate.

Poritz, pritzim (plural). (Uncertain etymology, possibly Slavic). The landlord; nearly all *shtetl* Jews rented from Gentile landlords.

Rebbe. The spiritual leader of a Hasidic group or community.

Ruah. That portion of the human Self that is intermediate in nature between the *nefesh* and *neshamah.* The *ruah* dissipates shortly after bodily death.

Ruah Hakodesh. Holy spirit.

Rav. Rabbi; traditionally known for his Talmudic mastery.

S'gulah. A charm or amulet given by a rebbe to a Hasid; such a charm was seen to possess healing, guarding, or enriching powers.

Shalom Bayit. Harmony in the home.

Shekinah. The female aspect to the deity. The *Shekinah* is described as dwelling amongst holy persons but as being an exile from its own Source.

Sheva B'rakhot. Literally, "seven blessings"; these are seven blessings that are pronounced each day during the wedding feast week.

Shtetl. (Yiddish) Small town, village.

Sihot. Informal discourses.

Simcha. Joy, happiness.

Talmud. The summary of the Judaic oral law, compiled in writings by sages in Palestine and Babylonia. Completed about 500 C.E., it exists in two editions, one for each center of world Judaism of the time. Some Hasidic figures downplayed the significance of the Talmud and thereby incurred the wrath of the *Mitnaggedim.*

Tanya. "It Has Been Taught," the title of the major theoretical work by Rabbi Schneur Zalman of Liady. Its chief section was first published in 1796 and has been intensively studied by Lubavitch Hasidim and others ever since.

Targum. Translations, usually from Hebrew to Aramaic.

Teshuvah. Repentance, or more broadly, return and ascent to one's divine source of origin.

Tiqun. Literally, "restoring to order, repairing"; a counsel on how to make reparations and restitution.

Tohu. Confusion, chaos.

Torah. In a narrow sense, the Pentateuch. More widely, Torah is understood to comprise the twenty-four books of the Bible and the Talmud.

Yehidah. In Kabbalistic terminology, the highest portion of the soul.

Yehidut. Literally, "one-ing"; a Hasid's private encounter with his rebbe.

Yeshivah, yeshivot (plural). House of Study.

Yezer Hara. The evil inclination.

Yoshev Ohel. Literally, "sitting in the tent"; a person who devotes his life to study and contemplation.

Yungerman. (Yiddish) A recently married young man.

Zaddik, zaddikim. "Righteous One." In Hasidism, the *zaddik* is the spiritual leader of the community and is regarded as an intermediary between it and the divine world.

Zohar. The "Book of Splendor," which first appeared in late thirteenth-century Spain. It is the "bible" of the Kabbalah and its most influential work. Ascribed to Simeon bar Yochai of the second century by traditionalists, scholars today attribute it to Moses de Leon, who is said to have composed most of it in the 1280s and 1290s.

BIBLIOGRAPHY

If you have enjoyed this book you may wish to read the more detailed study of the *yehidut*. The original dissertation offers a more inclusive treatment of this fascinating subject, as well as documenting the full range of Hasidic sources consulted and cited in this research. You may order the original study from University Microfilms International, 300 Zeeb Road, Ann Arbor, Michigan 48106. The work is replete with a thorough list of references and footnotes. It is listed under, *The Encounter* (Yehidut) by Zalman M. Schachter, #7815256, Hebrew Union College—Doctor of Hebrew Letters, 1968.

B'nai Or, a nonprofit Jewish fellowship, serves the American Jewish community by providing a variety of programs and activities to improve the quality of individual and communal Jewish experience. Created in 1962, B'nai Or combines traditional Torah study, Kabbalah, Hasidism, meditation, song, prayer, and current techniques of humanistic and transpersonal psychology. B'nai Or also maintains an extensive collection of books and tape recordings related to these concerns. For more information, please write or call: B'nai Or, 6723 Emlen Street, Philadelphia, Pennsylvania 19119, (215) 849-5385.

The following additional sources have been helpful in preparation of this book:

Ehrmann, Naftali Hertz. *The Rav.* Translated by Karen Paritzky. Jerusalem: Feldheim, 1977.

Hoffman, Edward. *The Way of Splendor.* Boulder, Colorado: Shambhala Publications, 1981.

Hoffman, Edward. "The Kabbalah: Its Implications for Humanistic Psychology." *Journal of Humanistic Psychology*, Winter 1980, *20* (1), 33–47.

Jacobs, Louis. *Hasidic Prayer.* New York: Schocken, 1978.

Jacobs, Louis. *Hasidic Thought.* New York: Schocken, 1976.

Kaplan, Aryeh. *The Light Beyond.* Brooklyn, New York: Maznaim, 1981.

Klapholtz, Yisroel Yaakov. *Tales of the Baal Shem Tov*, volumes 1–3. Translated by Abigail Nadav and Sheindel Weinbach. Bnei-Brak, Israel: Yisroel Klapholtz, Rechov Belz 3, 1970–1971.

Minkin, Jacob S. *The Romance of Hassidism.* North Hollywood, California: Wilshire, 1971.

Rabbi Nachman's Wisdom. Translated by Aryeh Kaplan. Brooklyn, New York: Aryeh Kaplan, 1976.

Schachter, Zalman M. *Fragments of a Future Scroll.* Germantown, Pennsylvania: Leaves of Grass Press, 1975.

Schochet, Jacob Immanuel. *The Great Maggid.* Brooklyn, New York: Kehot Publication Society, 1978.

Zohar, volumes 1–5. Translated by Harry Sperling and Maurice Simon. London: Soncino Press, 1931–1934.

APPENDIX

TRAINING
THE REBBES
OF THE FUTURE

In these tumultuous times, people have a very great need for genuine healers of the spirit. Many rebbes will have to be trained to provide meaningful counsel. Yet, within virtually every form of spiritual training, certain aspects are more essential than others. So, too, with Hasidism. What then are the key characteristics one must acquire to be a true rebbe? The following seven traits seem most crucial to us:

(1) An experience of kinship with other beings on the planet—that is, a sense of compassion transcending the bounds of ego, time and place.

(2) An inner "awakening," in which one encounters the realm of the transcendent, however fleeting or incomplete that sacred moment may be.

(3) A thorough understanding—and working through—of one's own emotional imbalances. In this way, one will be less likely to project his/her problems onto those seeking advice.

(4) A firm "grounding" in one's own body awareness, so that one is comfortable—neither anxious nor obsessed—about dealing with the sensual world.

(5) A comprehensive philosophical-intellectual training, enabling one to grasp a variety of "reality-maps" of consciousness, not just the everyday reality of human existence.

(6) A well-developed sense of intuition, so that one knows when to discard rote principles and generalizations and rely instead on personal hunches.

(7) An active participation in a community or network, so that one can engage in honest soul-searching with others as friendly critics and guides.

Edward Hoffman received his doctorate in psychology from the University of Michigan. He is currently Clinical Director and Director of Psychology at Hollywood Pavilion in Hollywood, Florida. Dr. Hoffman serves as an adjunct professor at Nova University and maintains a private practice as a clinical psychologist. He is the author of *The Way of Splendor: Jewish Mysticism and Modern Psychology* and coauthor of *The Man Who Dreamed of Tomorrow: A Conceptual Biography of Wilhelm Reich*. In addition, he is the editor-in-chief of *Four Worlds Journal*, a new periodical devoted to Jewish mysticism and its contemporary relevance for today. It may be ordered through: *Four Worlds Journal*, 1415 S.W. 21st Avenue, Fort Lauderdale, Florida 33315.

Studio of Hollywood Hills

Born in Poland, raised in Vienna, Zalman M. Schachter was ordained as a Lubavitch-trained rabbi in Brooklyn and for more than thirty-five years has brought the Hasidic way to men and women around the globe. He received a master's degree in psychology from Boston University and a doctorate from Hebrew Union College. Reb Zalman has served the Jewish community in many ways: as a congregational rabbi, a Hebrew school principal, a university professor, and a spiritual guide for individuals and communities throughout North America and Israel. From 1956–1975 he was Professor of Religion and Head of the Department of Near Eastern and Judaic Studies at the University of Manitoba in Canada. Since 1975, he has been Professor in Jewish Mysticism and Psychology of Religion at Temple University in Philadelphia. He has published over 150 articles and translations. His books include *Fragments of a Future Scroll: Hasidism for the Aquarian Age* and *The First Step: A Guide for the New Jewish Spirit*.